PSYCHOLOGY LIBRARY EDITIONS:
PERSONALITY

I0130630

Volume 15

THE NATURE OF
HUMAN PERSONALITY

THE NATURE OF
HUMAN PERSONALITY

G. N. M. TYRRELL

Routledge
Taylor & Francis Group
LONDON AND NEW YORK

First published in 1954 by George Allen and Unwin Ltd

This edition first published in 2019
by Routledge
2 Park Square, Milton Park, Abingdon, Oxon OX14 4RN

and by Routledge
52 Vanderbilt Avenue, New York, NY 10017

Routledge is an imprint of the Taylor & Francis Group, an informa business

British Library Cataloguing in Publication Data
A catalogue record for this book is available from the British Library

ISBN: 978-0-367-03112-1 (Set)
ISBN: 978-0-429-05756-4 (Set) (ebk)
ISBN: 978-0-367-15147-8 (Volume 15) (hbk)
ISBN: 978-0-367-15163-8 (Volume 15) (pbk)
ISBN: 978-0-429-05539-3 (Volume 15) (ebk)

Publisher's Note
The publisher has gone to great lengths to ensure the quality of this reprint but points out that some imperfections in the original copies may be apparent.

Disclaimer
The publisher has made every effort to trace copyright holders and would welcome correspondence from those they have been unable to trace.

The Nature of
Human Personality

G. N. M. TYRRELL

FOREWORD BY PROFESSOR H. H. PRICE

George Allen and Unwin Ltd
RUSKIN HOUSE · MUSEUM STREET · LONDON

Printed in Great Britain
in 12 point Bembo type
at the University Press
Aberdeen

FOREWORD

ALL students of psychical research are familiar with the work of
the late G. N. M. Tyrrell. The distinction of his writing, the
breadth and fairness of his mind, the originality of his contribu-
tions both to the experimental side of the subject and to the
theoretical interpretation of the facts, had made him one of the
world's leading authorities in this difficult and fascinating field.

This book was written in the last year or two of his life. When
he died in October 1952 the manuscript was almost complete,
and only a very little editing has been necessary, chiefly in the last
chapter. As he himself explains in the preface, it was intended to
be a sequel to *The Personality of Man* (1946). It is also, in a way, a
sequel to his earlier work *Homo Fabor* (1951). Its main aim is not
to present fresh evidence, but to assess the significance of the
evidence we already have. What light do paranormal phenomena
throw on the nature of human personality and the relations of
human personality to the rest of the universe? Tyrrell's answer
is that if rightly considered they alter our whole perspective
('perspective' is one of the key-words of the book). The paranormal facts which psychical research has revealed cannot just be
added to the 'normal' facts we already know. They demand a
revolution in our whole view of the world. Why do we call
them 'paranormal' at all? Because they conflict with certain
deep-rooted beliefs which all of us hold: beliefs so deep-rooted
that we seldom formulate them in words and are not ordinarily
even conscious of holding them. And that is also the reason why
we are all of us so reluctant to accept the paranormal facts. Their
consequences are too upsetting.

These beliefs make up what might be called the common-
sense outlook. What is their source? According to Tyrrell, they
have a *biological* origin. They are instinctive beliefs, instilled
into us by Nature for practical ends. A phrase he sometimes uses
for describing them is 'the adapted mind'. He thought that the
human mind, no less than the human body, has been adapted to
its environment in the course of evolution. The adapted mind
presents us with a simplified picture of the world and of ourselves,
much as a child's first history-book presents a simplified picture of
the historical facts. We instinctively believe that the world as we

v

perceive it by the senses is wholly objective; that there is nothing outside space and time; that the superficial self detectable by introspection and expressed in bodily behaviour is the whole self; that all the problems which we meet with are finally soluble. Of course this simplified picture has great biological utility. It helps us to live, and we could hardly live without it. Tyrrell does not deny that it corresponds in some degree to the facts, as the child's history-book does. But paranormal phenomena show that it is quite inadequate; and that is where their importance lies. They show us that human personality is far more complex and also far more baffling than common sense assumes. They suggest that the concepts of Space and Time do not apply to the whole of Reality; that even the most familiar material objects may have strange properties, of quite a different order from those revealed by our senses; that it would be nearer the truth to say *extunt omnia in mysterium* than to suppose that all problems are in principle soluble.

In this respect, Tyrrell argues, psychical research confirms the teachings of the mystics, who have always maintained that the perceptible world, and the empirical self too, are only appearance of a deeper reality inaccessible to the senses and the intellect. Indeed, he thinks that the 'intuitive' faculty which is present in its highest degree in the mystics is present in some degree in all men, along side of the adapted mind with its biologically-instilled instinctive beliefs. In the last chapter of the book there is a brief discussion of the relations between psychical research and religion from this point of view. Many readers will probably wish that this chapter had been longer.

H. H. PRICE

Our grateful thanks are due to Professor H. H. Price for his valuable advice and help in the preparation of this last book by G. N. M. Tyrrell.

C. M. TYRRELL.
G. M. JOHNSON.

PREFACE

THIS book is a sequel to *The Personality of Man*, which was published in the *Pelican Series* by Penguin Books Limited in 1946. Many letters were received from this and other countries containing questions prompted by the evidence cited in this book; and it seemed to the author that further consideration of this evidence was required.

The Personality of Man presented the factual side of psychical research, giving evidence which had been collected with rigorous care. Most of it was taken from the *Proceedings* and *Journals* of the Society for Psychical Research, a body which for the last seventy years has investigated the paranormal along scientific lines.

The present book has added a little to the evidence; but its principal object has been to consider its significance and to probe as deeply as possible into its meaning. The result of examining paranormal evidence is that certain principles of interest and importance have come to light. In the first place, the human faculties which give rise to the paranormal are seen to be universal. The paranormal therefore does not consist of mere oddities but of something universal, which is partly hidden. Everyone, for example, possesses in some degree the faculty of telepathy though only a few possess it markedly. It is a faculty which is world-wide in principle; but it is not reliable nor is it adapted for practical use like the ordinary senses. If perfected and made reliable it would not fit into life in the material world. Among the less civilized nations, it is, however, more widely operative than among the more highly sophisticated.

The tendency to regard the paranormal as a mere queer, isolated oddity arises because our minds have been developed for practical efficiency. The paranormal, if it came to the fore, would merely confuse and complicate the world of daily life. When, however, the mind is seeking for truth in deeper regions, the paranormal becomes an indicator of first importance. It gives a hint of the vast perspective of things which is hidden from the practical mind for practical reasons.

Psychical research also brings home another thing when we begin to grasp it: it shows that our attitude of mind plays a larger part in the acquisition of knowledge than we realize. In fact, the mind, for practical efficiency, is made to regard the things about it in a particular fashion; and a feature of great subtlety is introduced into this mental attitude. The fact that there *is* a mental attitude is concealed from the mind which possesses it; otherwise the serene confidence of the practical man would be disrupted.

This useful practical illusion loses its utility as soon as the mind, attaining a higher vantage-point, endeavours to discover the truth about its own situation. It has before it the difficult task of overcoming its own set habits. Here psychical research is a great help, for it reveals these set habits: the general attitude of mankind towards the paranormal reveals them: the tendency to ignore the paranormal and to explain it away reveals that there is something artificial and specialized in the human mind.

If these set habits can be overcome, the paranormal takes us still further and reveals two facts of paramount importance. One is that the ordinary common self of daily life is not the whole self, but is no more than a specialized abstraction from a far greater self, whose characteristics and scope go beyond our comprehension. The second is that the universe is similarly not solely composed of that which the senses and intellect can grasp, but extends indefinitely beyond our sensory limits, beyond space and time and beyond the reach of anything that can be grasped by the mind.

In this short book examination of the different branches of the paranormal will show that all alike converge towards these two great principles. And these principles are entirely opposed to the world-outlook of the present day, which is largely the product of science. They show that Materialism rests on a *subjective* basis; for it is the result of the mind's unconscious interpretation of facts in accordance with its own constitution.

This pointing of the different branches of the paranormal in one direction has inevitably led to a certain amount of repetition. The reader may regard this as unnecessary; but on the part of the author it is deliberate. For experience has shown that the mind,

urged by its innate impulses, will repeatedly reject these conclusions if they are not frequently reiterated.

Thus, the primary lesson which the paranormal has to teach
is this. Nature always urges us to turn *outwards* in the search for
truth; but if we wish to discover things that lie outside the field
of practical achievement, the essential thing is to look *within*.

CONTENTS

CHAPTER I

Psychology and Psychiatry

PSYCHOLOGY is one of the newer sciences; therefore the things
it will ultimately reveal are not yet as visible as they are in
the older sciences. One can, however, notice an important feature
at the outset. Experimental psychology has adopted the methods
of physical science and applied them to the study of the mind
without criticizing this procedure. Physics, chemistry, geology,
astronomy, etc., set out to analyse the physical universe; therefore
their primary aim is to be objective. In other words, they concentrate their attention on the data supplied by the human senses
and observe the external world with accuracy and constant
repetition until they have built up a valid picture of it. This
concentration on the spatial and temporal attributes of matter
directs these subjects more and more towards measurement and
mathematics.

Psychology entered the laboratory with this inheritance from
the physical sciences and endeavoured to explore the mind on
similar lines. Since the mind cannot be directly measured, quantitative methods had to be applied to reactions of the body as it
responded to mental stimuli. This method revealed facts which
were indeed related to the mind: it probed a certain distance into
that psycho-physical combination which we call man; but what
many psychologists did not realize is that in following the technique of physics they had embarked upon their research from a
specialized and not from a general standpoint. They had launched
out into the physical world *before* beginning to investigate the
mind; and hence imposed restrictions which a more introspective
method would not have done. It did not occur to them that it was
necessary to examine one's own mind and realize its peculiarities
before embarking on the study of mind in general.

The experimental psychologist would probably reply to this
by saying that in psychology he had adopted the only possible

line. To step into the external world, he would say, as a preliminary to studying the mind, is inevitable. Up to a certain point
this is true; but it is not wholly true. The main point is that, even
if it were the only way of exploring the mind, it is absolutely
essential, if we are not to be woefully misled, to recognize the
limited and specialized character of the tools we are using and to
make allowances for them. It should be recognized that this type
of psychology has adopted a *specialized* mode of approach, which
is impregnated with peculiar limitations.

If we are to form any reliable idea of the nature of mind (or,
indeed, of the ultimate nature of anything), it is necessary to see
it from an impartial standpoint. If we cannot do this at once,
we can at least leave the specialist's groove and look at it from
different, converging points of view, integrating these so as to
bring the object of our research into something like a true
perspective. But the type of psychologist I am considering does
not seem to be conscious of the highly special character of his
angle of approach: he does not say: I am looking at the human
mind from one particular point of view only, therefore I can
describe only one special aspect of it. He appears to think that
psychology gives him a central and all-inclusive picture, which he
identifies with the mind as it is in an absolute sense; and those who
hear his account for the most part acquiesce and hold the same
point of view. The result is that his picture of mind penetrates no
nearer to the final essence of mind than an astronomer's picture of
the sun would do if he examined nothing but reflected sunlight.

It is because the human senses and intellect have been developed along pragmatic lines for dealing practically with matter
that mind is seen only through its reactions with matter; and this
causes mind to be regarded either as an isolable entity, like a
material object, or else as a function of such an object. On
account of the specialized nature of our own minds, our reason is
easily deflected and led astray. It says: Wherever we look, we never
find mind in operation apart from the physical brain. Mind must
therefore be a causal effect of matter; or, if it is not, it must at any
rate be something that we can investigate by the methods which
are used in the physical sciences. But these exclusive alternatives

result from the fact that the scientist looks at things through a limited peep-hole.

The psychology of the laboratory has embarked upon a somewhat self-contradictory programme, for its aim is to explore the internal by external methods. But psychology, like every other science, has two distinct objects in view. One is to gain knowledge: the other is to evolve techniques which are useful in practice. It is the second objective which has always been by far the most successful in science.

During the last fifty years, psychology has launched out in a new direction and has developed a medical branch known as psychiatry, the roots of which may be traced back to the end of the eighteenth century, when Mesmerism began to attract attention. Mesmerism, afterwards called Hypnotism, blazed the trail for the new psychology by stepping across the boundary of the ordinarily conscious mind and entering a new and unexplored field. During the nineteenth century more and more attention was turned towards this field, but as one might have expected, it was explored more for its medical utility than to gain knowledge of the human being. It was investigated because it offered a means of curing mental disorders, which had their origin beyond the conscious boundary. Paul and Pierre Janet worked upon it in France during the 1880s ; Binet practised it a decade later. In 1903, F. W. H. Myers published his book, *Human Personality and its Survival of Bodily Death*, in which he developed his theory of the Subliminal Self. This theory was based, not on the evidence of medical psychology alone, for at that time it had not advanced far, but also on the collection of cases that had been made in the early days of psychical research. It was a wider theory than that constructed by the psychiatric branch of psychology. During the first third of the twentieth century, the work of Sigmund Freud attracted widespread attention. He was a pupil of Charcot, who had devoted himself to the investigation of hysteria, in the course of which he discovered that factors outside the conscious mind were responsible for this disorder. Some of these factors were found to have been suppressed from consciousness and thereby gave rise to conflicts in the subconscious region of the mind. The latter was designated by Freud the 'Unconscious'; and, for dealing with this region of the mind, he invented the technique of psycho-analysis, for which he became world famous.

It is important to remember that psychiatry has always been a medical technique rather than an exploratory branch of science. Hence it is bound to approach its subject from a highly special point of view. It does not stand back and survey the mind from various angles, which is a method essential for arriving at truth. One instance of this is provided by the creation of the vague term 'unconscious'. What does it mean? Is the 'unconscious' unconscious? What does one mean by 'an unconscious mental process'? Can a process which *is* unconscious be intelligibly called 'mental'? If so, the term 'mental' needs to be redefined. How far does the 'unconscious' extend? Has it a boundary? If so, where is its boundary? Does precognition take place in the 'unconscious'? If so, the 'unconscious' must transcend the precincts of time, as we know it.

The psychiatrist has not attempted to answer these questions but has concentrated on the cure of mental diseases. Therefore his statements about the nature of the human being and the apparent implication of his terms need not be taken too seriously. One psychiatrist, for example, said: 'The unconscious is merely a term which comprises everything that exists, that has existed, or that could exist beyond the range of this individual consciousness.'[1]

This kind of thing, as well as the universal conclusions drawn by Freud from his researches, brings to mind the story of the frog which tried to inflate itself into a bull. Psychiatry deals with only a fringe of the mind beyond normal consciousness: yet its investigations of dreams and complexes, and especially the wider work of C. G. Jung, have been of great value.

From the standpoint of an inquiry which endeavours to form an adequate conception of the human being, the important thing about psychiatry is that it has crossed the boundary of normal consciousness, and its crossing has been generally accepted; and it has added from its own point of view to the evidence that there

[1] Dr. H. Godwin Baynes, *Journal* Society for Psychical Research, Vol. xxx, p. 68.

is more beyond this boundary. Freud, at least in his early work, still regarded the normal consciousness as the centre of the human being and the 'unconscious' as being a rubbish-heap in the background. Myers, taking into account the more far-reaching evidence of psychical research, was struck by the fact that the subliminal self contains a goldmine as well as a rubbish-heap. The long history of intuition and inspiration, which is chiefly responsible for the intellectual progress of the human race, provides still more evidence that the mind extends far beyond the conscious boundary in a positive direction. Every original thinker receives his key-ideas from outside his conscious mind. Flashes of inspiration are far more effective than the logical process of academic reasoning. Poets, authors, musicians, scientists have owed most of their greatest works to this; while genius supplies an overpowering example of it. All that the psychiatrist has done is to take a first step across the boundary at a somewhat low level and to investigate what he immediately finds there.

If we abandon the view-point of the specialist and take a general survey, the common-sense assumption about the human being is reversed. Instead of seeing the normally conscious being as the centre of the self, and the subconscious or unconscious as no more than a marginal fringe, it shows that the centre of the human being lies beyond, and not on the near side of, the boundary of normal consciousness. The normal self is a highly specialized abstraction from the total human personality and is adapted for existence under very special circumstances. The nature of the whole being is far beyond the capacity of the intellect to grasp.

There are three features of normal consciousness which are of great importance for our whole inquiry. One is that the sphere of operation of the ordinary mind is extremely limited. The second is that it is for the most part conscious only of things which affect it in a practical manner. The third is that its degree of consciousness varies continually, passing up and down a graded scale from a narrow range at the bottom (which is the practical end) to a wider range when engaged in reflective thought.

Our awareness of what goes on in our bodies is extremely restricted. When we make use of our senses, we are aware only of their end-products. Of the complex processes which go on when we see, hear or touch, we are totally unaware. With muscular movement it is the same. We *will* that our hand shall go out and grasp an object; but all we are conscious of is that it does so. The immensely complicated series of processes that our will has set in motion make no impression on our awareness—the nerve-impulses, the exactly co-ordinated muscular contractions, the incredibly complicated activities of the brain-cells—all these we neither control nor know anything about. Yet they surely cannot be wholly mechanical: they are minutely regulated. How can mind be absent from the details of this regulating process? It has been *arranged* that our narrow band of practical conscious-ness shall be unaware of this regulating portion of the mind. All that the normally conscious mind is aware of is the willed effort and its result; and this means that it has been limited and adapted for practical ends.

This brings us to the second point. The ordinarily conscious mind is strictly conditioned in other ways, being adapted to common life as the glove to the hand. It is so conditioned that everything that is not necessary to become part of its awareness is withheld from its consciousness. Not only are the processes of per-ception, muscular action and all bodily functions withheld from view: it is so constituted that it instinctively turns a cold shoulder to anything likely to confuse its world or to distract its attention from practical efficiency. The unpopularity of such deeply probing subjects as philosophy or psychical research and the reduction of religion to mere outward and formal observance are examples of this.

The third point is that the mind flashes up and down its graded scale of awareness so rapidly that it does not realize that it is doing so. At the level of action the mind cannot reflect: it can do little more than react to sense-stimuli. Instantly it can, however, mount to a higher level of awareness; and then it is able to ponder over what sense-revelations mean. In a flash it has risen to a higher condition of consciousness. It has expanded. So there are ranges of being or selfhood even within the confines of ordinary conscious-ness; and beyond these confines the range continues.

Psychology points to two important things. In the first place, to the high degree of specialization which the practical portion of the mind has undergone while it was being adapted to the physical world. In the second place, to the fact that the practically adapted part does not include the whole. The mind is not a self-contained entity, neatly rounded off and confined within a rigid boundary. It is true that it has the appearance of being such; but the further psychology advances the more this is shown to be only an appearance. The appearance has been pre-arranged by nature to ensure simplicity throughout practical life. In truth, the self expands indefinitely beyond its empirical boundary, and in essence it is incomprehensible. If any physical analogy were applicable to the mind, it might be compared with the spectrum of light. All knowledge we have of it shows that it is far more like this than it is like an isolated and self-contained entity.

To realize that the mind or self is not something enclosed within the spatial boundary of the body is extremely important; but there is something else of equal importance. This is the way in which our true nature has been concealed from us. The innate tendency of the mind is to assume that everything is a detached entity, easily comprehensible by the human intellect. This assumption is justified so long as we are dealing with the practical side of life: that is why it has been instilled into the human mind and why we always take it for granted. The entire methodology of science reflects this characteristic of the mind, in spite of the fact that the advance of pure science gently but persistently unmasks it. And although psychology is a comparatively new science, this unmasking is making steady progress. The subtlety of our mental constitution and the importance of realizing it looms larger and larger the more we make progress. At last we begin to see that it is a universal principle underlying the whole of our conception of ourselves and of the universe. It is extremely subtle, for part of its very constitution is that it remains invisible so long as the mind remains at a low level of awareness.

An inkling of this mysterious, invisible factor which enters into our processes of reasoning, is supplied by reflection on the past history of man. Instinct plays a dominant role in the animal world; and as human beings arose out of that world, instinct played a major role in the formation of the human mind. To deny that we have inherited instincts from our primitive ancestors would be to fly in the face of truth. Instinct forms, in fact, the red and infra-red portions of the mental spectrum. Without it, the human mind would be quite inefficient in action. But the bands of the mental spectrum interpenetrate one another—that is why the spectrum of light is an imperfect analogy. Instinct does not remain at the bottom but rises and impregnates the mind at the level of intellect; but the subtle point is that it acts in a hypnotic manner, causing the conscious mind to be unaware that it is being acted upon. Nevertheless, as the level of awareness rises the power of instinct declines, and then it becomes easier to see through this quasi-hypnotic suggestion.

Instinct not only impregnates sense-perception: it flows into every department of practical life, and is responsible for the world's eternal troubles. War is prompted by instinct mingled with reason; and man brings vast suffering upon himself by acting in ways that pure reason would denounce. But all the while the clear light of reason, untrammelled by instinct, would reveal the insanity of actions prompted by the lower levels and would suggest easy methods of negotiating a satisfactory peace and of settling every kind of difficulty. The madness of actions prompted by the lower levels of the mind would then be as clear as daylight.

From our general standpoint, which is wider than that of the specialist, the salient achievement of psychology is this: by the use of recognized scientific methods it has crossed the boundary of normal consciousness and discovered that there is more of the self beyond. And we notice a remarkable and highly significant thing. Now that the Rubicon has been crossed and a more first-hand contact has been made with the mystery of being, the latter becomes less and less easy to define. The psychologist has opened an ever-widening vista: the apparently comprehensible begins to lapse into the incomprehensible, which is a sure sign of a step towards reality.

CHAPTER II

To what does Extra-Sensory Perception Point?

TURNING now to psychical research, the first question that arises concerns the significance of extra-sensory perception; for this is the most definite and fully confirmed branch of what is called the 'paranormal'. A brief summary of the evidence for it was given in chapters 6 to 15 in *The Personality of Man*. The evidence falls into two main groups, (1) spontaneous and (2) experimental. The spontaneous group consists of some hundreds of carefully collected cases sent in by members of the public and thoroughly examined by the Society for Psychical Research, and some by other similar bodies. Also many true statements have been uttered by mediums and taken down verbatim at the time, and these concern facts which the medium could not possibly have known by any normal means.

The experimental category includes tests of a qualitative nature, in which the agent looked at some object while the percipient, sometimes many miles away, noted down his impressions.

Also book-tests have been carried out, in which a medium has stated what was on a particular page in a book which was standing on a shelf in a house to which she had no access.[1]

During the last two decades quantitative experiments have been carried out based on the principle of guessing cards or simple objects, to which statistical evaluation can be applied. These experiments, carried out chiefly in America and England, run into thousands.

The evidence, when taken all together, is immensely strong; for the spontaneous cases were carefully sifted and examined before publication; the witnesses were often questioned personally and all relevant evidence was taken into account. The spontaneous precognitive cases, published by the Society for Psychical Research, amount to about two hundred.

[1] See *Proc.* S.P.R., Vol. xxxi, p. 242.

The quantitative experiments have the advantage that the like-lihood of chance, as an explanation of the results, can be calculated mathematically. The qualitative experiments, on the other hand, have the advantage of revealing a good deal more of the process. When the object is not a card or something of the kind, it can be seen how the percipient reaches some aspect of it or approaches it by association of ideas. This insight into the process protects the experimenter from making fictitious assumptions to which the card-experiments are likely to give rise, such as the view that extra-sensory perception is a kind of analogue to ordinary sense-perception, whose processes take place in the space-time world.

Examples of both qualitative and quantitative evidence for extra-sensory perception were given in *The Personality of Man*, and it is our business in this book to consider their significance. But before doing so, it seems worth while to give an account of some rather different experiments carried out by myself, which were omitted from *The Personality of Man* for lack of space.[1]

The apparatus used for these experiments was electrically operated and the results recorded automatically. I sat at a small table with the controlling apparatus in front of me and behind it a wooden screen about three feet square. The percipient sat at a similar table about five feet away from mine with her part of the apparatus in front of her and behind it a similar screen. We sat so that both the screens were between us and we could not see each other; nor could we see each other's apparatus.

In front of me were five keys, rendered soundless by mercury contacts, and an automatic recorder of the results. In front of the percipient were five little boxes with overlapping spring lids, each containing an electrical pea-lamp. When I pressed a key, it lit the corresponding lamp in one of the boxes, and the experiment consisted in the percipient trying to open the box in which was the lighted lamp. All results were recorded automatically on a morse-tape machine from which a strip of paper emerged driven by clockwork. On the strip, successes were recorded as double dashes and failures as single dashes. When the percipient opened a box with a lighted lamp in it, a double dash was automatically

[2] See *Proc.* S.P.R., Vol. xliv, Part 147, pp. 99-166.

recorded; and if any of the four boxes without a lighted lamp inside were opened, a single dash resulted. Thus there was a permanent record of every trial.

Every precaution was taken. The box-lids closed tightly on to velvet and were tested in the dark to make sure that no ray of light escaped. The keys were silent. An automatic device was installed which ensured that if more than one box were opened at a time, no success could be recorded. An additional device was sometimes employed which precluded hypothetical light-leakage or the still more hypothetical suggestion that the box with the lighted lamp in it might be slightly warmer than the others (for the experiments were conducted at the rate of one a second). The percipient merely tipped up the overlapping box-lids with her finger as fast as she could, and they instantly snapped down again and were held tightly by their springs. This additional device arranged that when a key was pressed the lamp-circuit was *selected*, but the lamp was not lit: the act of opening the box lit it. This experiment seemed, therefore, to involve precognition.

This electrical apparatus gave opportunity for trying different kinds of experiments, and often for trying them without the knowledge of the percipient. When, for example, I pressed the keys, which I always did in a strictly random order by using figures taken from logarithmic tables, I knew which lamp I was lighting. But a commutator was inserted between the keys and the lamps so that, by pressing an additional key, the commutator revolved quickly, stopping in an unknown position and connecting the lamps to the keys in an unknown order. Thus selection of the boxes by thought-transference was eliminated. I also installed a mechanical device which could take the place of the keys and would light the lamps in an unknown order; and this order could also be changed by pressing another key. Interesting experiments could thus be carried out which could not be done by the guessing of cards.

Some conclusive precognitive experiments were done in another way. The percipient selected a box and opened it before any lamp had been lit. About half a second later I pressed a key, which lit one of the lamps unknown to me, for the commutator was always in action and the connections between keys and lamps unknown. The successes and failures were recorded automatically on the morse recorder. In this experiment the two dashes marking a success were not quite opposite to one another, the dash made by opening the box beginning earlier than the dash made by pressing the key. This displacement was an automatic proof that the key was pressed after the box had been opened.

One experiment carried out under these conditions consisted of 2255 trials of which 539 were successes. The successes were thus 88 above chance-expectation. This, when worked out by the statistical formulae, gave odds against chance of over 100,000 to 1.

An argument against the view that these experiments were actually precognitive might perhaps be brought forward as follows. It might be said that the percipient clairvoyantly 'saw' the table of randomized numbers in front of me and which I used to press the keys in a random order, although they were hidden from her by double screens. She then detected clairvoyantly the complicated wiring of the commutator, which was enclosed in a thick wooden box so as to be inaudible when operated. The commutator connections were frequently altered during experiments; but it might be said that the percipient had detected or worked out beforehand which of the lamps would be lighted, although this working out was unsuccessful in the case of failures.

It is important to realize that 'clairvoyance' in the sense of a direct perception of physical objects without the use of the sense-organs, is a purely theoretical conception and is unsupported by any positive evidence. In fact, it is inherently contradictory. Suppose, for example, that a pack of cards has been shuffled in an unknown order and that the percipient correctly guesses more of the cards than can be attributed to chance, why should we assume that the *physical* properties of the cards are being perceived by a faculty which is akin to sight? If, say, the fourth card in the pack is correctly guessed (or known), how does 'clairvoyance' operate? The first three cards must be transparent to the faculty while the fourth card is opaque! How can any faculty of perception render a physical object transparent or opaque to suit its convenience? This literal theory of 'clairvoyance' is obviously absurd. Besides, spontaneous cases of apparent 'clairvoyance' also point against the view that the faculty is in any way akin to sight; for in some of these cases the scene of the event is perceived some hours after it has occurred. It is only the quantitative experiments which suggest this literal theory of 'clairvoyance' because of their uninformative nature; the qualitative experiments and the spontaneous cases point in the opposite direction and indicate that so-called 'clairvoyance' does not take place in the physical world at all. Its source is outside that world and unknown to us. To take the physical hypothesis of 'clairvoyance' seriously is therefore unscientific and irrational.

One interesting point in the experiments with the electrical machine is worthy of mention. The trials were conducted so rapidly that the percipient's hand had begun to move towards the box that it was going to open before the key had been pressed in the great majority of the experiments. It is therefore questionable whether most of the experiments were not in fact precognitive, whether they were intended to be so or not. I have been struck by the fact that all evidence of a paranormal kind seems to pass over the border of precognition with indifference, as if there were no real boundary there.

Many experiments done under different conditions with this electrical machine gave very high odds against chance. For myself, at any rate, they proved the existence of extra-sensory perception up to the hilt; and the work of others fully endorsed it, as was shown in *The Personality of Man*, chapter 5.

The guessing of cards which are looked at one by one by an agent suggests at first sight the passage of thought from his brain or conscious mind to the brain or conscious mind of the percipient. But experiments of a qualitative kind throw more light on the process and do not endorse the superficial impression given by card-guessing. Two examples from a series of experiments carried out a long time ago serve as an illustration of this. For this purpose the lapse of time does not invalidate them. The question of the part played by chance can only be assessed by reading the whole series.[1]

[1] *Proc.* S.P.R., Vol. xxi, pp. 60-75.

Miss C. Miles was the agent and Miss H. Ramsden the percipient. They were twenty miles apart at the time.

On October 20th, 1905, Miss Miles concentrated her attention on the idea of SPHINX. On the same day at 7 p.m. Miss Ramsden recorded her impression as follows:

Cossack

Cross

Compass (?)

Luzac (the publisher)

Luxor in Egypt

Here I gave up in despair, then suddenly came the word Whistle!

This I believed to be correct.   H. R.

Again on October 20th, 1906, the following episode happened. *Miss Miles writes as follows :—*

'Blaise Castle, Henbury. On Saturday, October 20th, I had tea with the Bishop of Bristol. He showed me all over the grounds [and] chapel; there was a cross.

'I wished you to see the bishop.—C. M.'

From Miss Ramsden:—

'Ardverikie, Kingussie, N.B., Saturday, October 20th. I believe you forgot all about it!

'6.30 p.m., a necklace and a ring seen as two circles, one inside the other.

'7.30 p.m. A.M.W. letters intertwined like a monogram, church steeple, a fish, a star, a cup of tea, something round . . . egg-shaped, a ball of pink string, a cockle-shell "latme", Bishop Latimer, Archbishop. . . .—H. R.'

From Miss Harford:—

'Blaise Castle, Henbury. Saturday, October 20, 1906. I sent Miss Miles off at four o'clock to the Bishop of Bristol's Palace in a pony cart driven by a groom. She found the Bishop in and had tea there.

'Something round, egg-shaped, may mean a very curious

Arab ring which I wear, and which has a history and we have talked about it a good deal. It has a large, dark red stone, something like a cornelian or jaspar with heavy old-fashioned setting, and the shape of the stone is like the pointed end of an egg.—CHARLOTTE HARFORD.'

These descriptions do not suggest the flashing of an idea from mind to mind through space. They suggest the uprising of an idea from the subconscious to the conscious. They suggest that the idea is there in the background all the time and is trying to find its way into consciousness by selecting ideas at the conscious level that are more and more closely associated with it. The process is strongly reminiscent of the description given by Gurney in the Willett script,[1] of the way in which mediumistic messages are shepherded through to the level of consciousness. Association may go along a wrong track and lead to failure; or else quite separate ideas, such as 'Whistle' may come in from an unknown source. But the method did get as far as 'Luxor' when the object was 'Sphinx', and 'Bishop' when the agent was thinking of the Bishop of Bristol. There is a tendency to go off onto side-lines that are linked with the main idea, such as the egg-shaped stone in the ring. These spreading processes are not very suitable for statistical evaluation.

The work done in psychical research on the faculty known as extra-sensory perception, when regarded as a whole, brings to light two important facts. The first is that the evidence for the existence of this faculty is incontrovertible. The second is that it does not consist of an extra sense akin to seeing, touching, hearing, etc. It is not something which makes a direct response to physical stimuli; nor does it operate in the physical world. It is not the sort of thing that can be investigated to the bottom by physical science. All the evidence shows that the extra-sensory information rises to consciousness from the subconscious region, or the unconscious or extra-conscious or whatever term we choose to employ for the extended region of the self which lies beyond the restricted region of the self in everyday life.

[1] See Chap. III, pp. 30-33 below.

The source and origin of this information is probably not in time as we know it—not, that is to say, in the kind of time in which physical processes take place—for extra-sensory information about present, past or future events shows no sign of crossing the kind of boundary which separates them in this the past, present and future, the physical world. All points to the view that the world extends beyond the limits of the sense-field: also it points to an extension of ourselves beyond what in practical life we are impelled to regard as the whole of us. In this outward pointing to a vast beyond lies the significance of extra-sensory perception. It is a thing of great importance; but the rational mind tries to reject or belittle it. At the same time we must remember that the rational mind, unless it rises to a high level of intuition, is swayed by instinct. For example, Dr. A. C. Ewing, in a lecture on *Reason and Intuition* (British Academy 1941), said: 'But now the conclusion strongly suggested to very many minds is that, while we may use reason as a reliable instrument to argue from given ultimate premisses to conclusions based on them, these premisses are themselves merely instinctive beliefs with no possible rational justification, the mere product of evolution or of feeling.' This is why extra-sensory perception has not been regarded as supplying information which is of cardinal importance for science and philosophy.

Extra-sensory perception opens a door. It indicates that the world we live in is not the whole universe or even complete in itself. It shows it to be continuous with an extension of reality lying far beyond the range of our senses. The instinctive urge to cling to the ordinary world and to reject evidence for the existence of anything beyond is deeply rooted in the primitive mind of all humanity. Its origin is pragmatic, for it was evolved to promote practical efficiency and to make the external world appear simple; it was not designed to lead the mind to ultimate truth. Also, our minds are so constituted that they forcibly persuade us to believe that our senses show us the whole of reality; and they rebel against any evidence which threatens to reveal the contrary.

CHAPTER III

The Problem of Mental Mediumship

PSYCHIATRY has crossed the border from the conscious to the unconscious; but psychical research has crossed it too and has explored further. One reason why psychical research is particularly illuminating is that it shows that the mind or self beyond the empirical boundary of consciousness amounts to a great deal more than the mere limbo of repressed desires to which psychiatry points.

In *The Personality of Man* it was pointed out that carefully conducted sittings with mediums belonging to the mental category showed that all claim to be producing direct communications from the dead, but that such communications vary a great deal in quality. They are, in fact, *graded.* The lower grades (which are the commonest) contain much verbosity and often little sense; but here and there facts about the dead person who claims to be communicating shoot up among the padding as if coming through from a remote background; and characteristic things emerge which the medium could not normally have known. This points to the view that we should not jump to any cut and dried and final explanation until we have examined all the grades and qualities of mediumship and have got the problem into perspective.

The psychologist is not, as a rule, inclined to do this, for he inherits the scientific tradition which is based on the specialized character of the human mind and makes every question appear to be finally answerable. He assumes that every problem will rapidly converge to a final answer although pursued in isolation. The naïve spiritualist also follows a similar path, maintaining that the dead person is there in the simple sense in which a human being in this world speaks from the other end of a telephone.

An example of low grade mediumistic material is provided by the following brief abstract from a sitting of my own. The letter T indicates myself; and the letter C the medium's control.

C: Father, father. I hear someone say father, father.

T: Yes. That is right; that means someone is coming.

C: Yes. That is right. Such a nice young man too.

T: Oh yes, do you know him?

C: He has got nice eyes like you.

T: Oh, yes, yes. Perhaps he will say who he is.

C: Yes he will in a minute, I think. Laughs with his eyes. Smiles with his eyes. I see him.

T: Yes.

C: There is also your mother.

T: Yes.

C: She tells me she is your mother. She is nodding her head in agreement. She is saying no words. It is as if two or three come together to see you and I feel them lending strength.

T: Will you give them my greeting?

C: They hear you.

T: I am very glad to hear they are there.

C: I hear the name ROBERT spoken. [The name ROBERT means nothing to me.]

T: Yes.

C: I wouldn't worry too much about the names because they put them in at the oddest times and they may not be to do with the people I am speaking of, you see.

C (In a whisper): I so much want. . . . Halloa, Halloa, are you there? Halloa, are you there?

T: Yes I am here. Yes I can hear you.

C: Yes, Yes, you have lost hold again. It is all right. I am talking to him.

T: Yes I heard you speaking to me just now.

C: Now I hear them say mother, but it is not your mother. I gather it is a mother still here, still alive.

This sort of vague patter continues at great length without conveying anything definite. But at a higher level it is interspersed by flashes of definite information, which are often not only true but also characteristic of the purporting communicator. These give the impression of shooting through from another source. Examples are given in *The Personality of Man* chapter 22. At the highest level, the communications become clear and definite and differ entirely from the low grade type.

It is often asked why, if these are the dead communicating with the living, they do not tell us about the conditions in which they exist and give a clear description of the world they live in. Even a partial realization of our own situation in this world shows this question to be extremely naïve, for it ignores the fact that our minds are only capable of grasping knowledge of the particular kind they are suited to, and that our vocabulary is adapted to that kind of knowledge. Anything that does not conform to our specialized ways of thinking appears to our minds bizarre and is tossed aside as trash. A question of this kind does, in fact, reveal something of cardinal significance about ourselves, for it shows that our minds are so constructed that they take it for granted that they can grasp everything in the universe. The basic fact which the mind is so incapable of realizing is that the world we live in is no more than a tiny corner of the whole; for the very roots of the mind have been impregnated by Nature with the assumption that this world *is* the whole.

When we approach the difficult question of what mediumistic communications imply, we should not allow ourselves to reject without examination anything that has a surface-appearance of being trivial and childish; for anything which lies outside our common experience is likely to give rise to contempt. For this reason it is worth while to devote considerable space to communications on the highest level which claim to emanate from the dead. They pose a different problem; at any rate they give us reason to pause and reject any quick and easy psychological solution.

In chapter 18 of *The Personality of Man* a few examples were given of the automatic scripts of Mrs. Willett, which are the best examples of high level communications known to me. It is worth while devoting a good deal of space to a consideration of these high grade communications.

Mrs. Willett was one of the small and scattered group of ladies who practised automatic writing in the early part of this century in connection with the cross-correspondence.[1] Mrs. Willett, after a time, used to lapse into a peculiar state of consciousness as she wrote, unlike that of the ordinary mediums, for she had no 'control' and her normally conscious-self did not disappear. Edmund Gurney, who had been an extremely active worker in psychical research in its early days, died in 1888. He was one of the principal communicators through Mrs. Willett and in the course of a series of most interesting scripts he describes the process by which, from his point of view, communications are produced and externalized. These show Mrs. Willett as a rather inefficient go-between, who had to be coaxed and educated in the technique of communicating by a small group of deceased persons who had been vitally interested in psychical research during their lifetimes. One of the group was F. W. H. Myers, who died in 1901. He spoke as follows in one of Mrs. Willett's early scripts of 1909: 'I am trying experiments with you to make you hear without writing therefore as it is I Myers who do this deliberately do not fear or wince when words enter your consciousness or subsequently when such words are in the script. On the contrary it will be the success of my purpose if you recognise in yr. script phrases you have found in your consciousness. I know this must be for a while disconcerting and be filled with the fear of that eternal SS (*subliminal self*) which I hope we have succeeded in dethroning to some extent. Therefore be agreeing to be disconcerted and do not analyse whence these impressions, which I shall in future refer to as Daylight Impressions, come from, they are parts of a psychic education framed by me for you. . . .'[2] The " Daylight Impression " was afterwards referred to by the initial letters D.I.

Myers's hope that the subliminal self, as the supposed originator of the messages, has to some extent been 'dethroned' is a reference to the Cross Correspondences, referred to in chapter 17 of *The Personality of Man*. These were apparently to disprove

[1] See Chapter 17, *The Personality of Man*.
[2] *Proc.* S.P.R. Vol. xliii, p. 51.

the view that they originated from the subliminal selves of living persons. It consisted of a central theme distributed to the various automatists in fragments which did not make sense by themselves but which did make sense when put together.

Edmund Gurney, however, was the ostensible sender of a great many of the communications through Mrs. Willett, and he endeavoured to explain how the communications were sent. His explanation was not completely clear, for Mrs. Willett had difficulty in passing on what he said, as the following example shows. But the process was very complex, so that one can understand that nothing very difficult and certainly nothing beyond experience of a terrestrial kind could find its way through this restricted channel.

The following communication came on June 4th, 1911. The late Lord Balfour was present and the initials G.W.B. refer to him.

> Oh he says something French, . . . *pas qui coûte.*
> Oh yes, I know—I'm trying I will try.
> He says say how you feel.   (Oh I'm all right.)
> I'm far, I'm far.
> He says, I want to speak—and he says, what I'm going to say is not to be taken as applying to D.I.[1] when the communication is more direct and simpler, and he says, not to be taken as applying to all sensitives or even to all phenomena of any given sensitive. But it's an attempt to show how in some cases some scripts are produced.
> The descending chain—telepathy—inspiration—telepathy—selection. Oh he says, What thought is implied by the words 'mutual selection'?
> Oh he says, is he there? (*G.W.B.:* Yes, I'm here.)
> Does it reach him? (*G.W.B.:* Yes, I hear quite well.)
> I want to make a shot at a partial definition of what constitutes mediumship.
> That organisation in which the capacity for—what an odd word—

---

[1] 'Daylight Impressions', see p. 20, above.

Oh, Edmund, say it slowly—*excursus* is alive to the capacity for definite selection. Then finally the possession of as it were a vent, through which the knowledge can emerge.

Oh he says, there's a line of Tennyson's I'm thinking of—lies open unto me.

And all things he says like that, he says I don't repeat.

I thought I'd said it—I wonder where I am. He says, don't lose the thread.

Oh he says, what I'm going to say now may lead to some misunderstanding according as whether the right or the wrong deductions are drawn from it.

It's something like this. [Pause]

Say that after—Oh! how difficult it is—say that after deliberation a certain theme is selected. Then he says something in German—*motif*—to be got through various channels. I'm only speaking now of the process of selection, he says, and in so far as that's concerned I'm limited to the contents of the conscious and unconscious self.

Oh he says, Gerald—Oh he says like that. He's calling someone. Nobody answers—he keeps on calling someone. He says Gerald. Oh he keeps on calling. Oh! he says where is Gerald?

(*G.W.B.:* I'm here.)

Oh he says, does he hear? How can I know that he hears?

(*G.W.B.:* All right, I'm hearing perfectly.)

Oh I see him so plainly. [Remark by Mrs. Willett.]

He says to me Don't fail me—go on, go back to where you left off—about the mind.

Mind, he says, was the last word. [Refers to conscious and unconscious self.] He says Remember I am distinctly ruling out the thoughts suggested by the words telepathy and inspiration.

Oh he says, Well then I look over the available factors—oh, and see what will serve. Oh he says, it isn't only I who select Oh he says, now you've got it. There's another field for selection—and it's such part of my mind, I, Gurney, as she can have access to. Oh he says, What part? Why? Oh, I've missed a word—something something limited to—then I've skipped something, but I hear him say thoughts potentially. Oh he says, put it another way. Having access to my mind her selection is chiefly limited to that which can naturally link onto human incarnate thought. Oh he says, I wish I could get that word *potential* rightly used. I'm not saying it's limited to the actual but to the potential content. Oh he says, does he see what I'm driving at?

(*G.W.B.*: I think I do and no doubt I shall understand still better when I read it over.)

He says, that's where the gamble comes in. How will it be used, the knowledge supernormally gained? Now then, you have present in the whole self the matter from which I selected, plus the matter supernormally acquired from me. Now comes the weaving. Oh he says, That's where subliminal activity comes in. Oh he says, it's a dangerous weapon, yet we can't do without it.

Often there is a fairly long period of—don't get that word—it contains a *g* and an *s* and a *t* and an *n*. [G.W.B. suggests *gestation* but no notice is taken of this.] Say incubation he says, and then comes the uprush. And then, he says, now I must bring in telepathy as the guiding influence. He says this process is only one among a great variety. Oh he says, We must experiment—he says, so much is unmapped.

Oh, and he says, the waste of material when we keep on hammering at one point—approaching it from every—can't read that word—of the compass only to find that the point had been grasped and that we might have passed on to new matter.

Oh he says, I can't see your mind, Gerald, but I can feel you in some dim way through her. He says, It's a sort of lucky bag, her mind to me—when I'm not shut out from it.

He says I think I got some things I wanted said about selection. It's the thought of its being as it were a mutual process that I wanted driven home.

Oh he says, now say this for me. He says, you want to foster in sensitives a sort of dual attitude—belief in their capacity.

Oh! say it slowly—I'm so tired, I'm so tired—Oh I'm

climbing. Oh! I'm climbing. Belief, Oh I will, I will say it—belief in their capacity to have access to the mind of the communicator together with a wholesome sense of discrimination in regard to the expressions—not right—regard to something to which that access leads—productions.

Oh he says, you mayn't know it, there's a natural bent to extreme scepticism here.

Oh he says, there are such a lot of things I want to tell you, and there's the longing to know when one has struggled how far one has succeeded in making oneself—Oh he says, I mustn't go much further now.

Oh he says, don't give me up Gerald—help me—and help her.

Oh I can't go on, I'm so tired.

Oh he says, only one more thing—only one more thing for him.

He says it over and over. I'm trying (almost sobs).

Being is antecedent to—Oh he says, you've not got the word I want but say it—it'll suggest—Yes, that's it, action.

Oh that's done. [A pause; after which waking stage follows.][1]

Lord Balfour summarizes the gist of these communications as follows:

(1) The choice of a theme;
(2) The selection of material relevant to the theme by the sensitive from the mind of the communicator, and probably also by the communicator from the mind of the sensitive;
(3) a period of 'incubation', often a long one, during which there comes into play an operation described as 'weaving', and consisting in some kind of subliminal activity;
(4) actual production of script, involving selection by the communicator from the 'available factors' in the mind of the sensitive, and the bringing in of telepathy as a 'guiding influence'.

[1] *Proc.* S.P.R., Vol. xliii, pp. 232-5.

The first, third and fourth stages are but briefly indicated in the D.I. we are now considering, but further light is thrown upon them in later sittings, to which I shall presently have to call attention.[1]

The chief factors employed in constructing the messages coming through Mrs. Willett, and in getting them externalized, are described by Gurney in further D.Is.[2]

Telepathy, The following D.I. was obtained on September 24th, 1910, in which Sir Oliver Lodge (O.J.L.) acted as recorder:

(*Gurney speaking*): Telepathy isn't involuntary, it's—I'm going to do it like this—what's the word? Propulsion—you watch the receipt.

Mrs. W.: Now he's as if holding my hand, it's as if having a tooth out, youve got to set your teeth and go through with it. He says James and another name.

E.G.: Now she's got it, and you watch it coming up. It's got into the subliminal.

Mrs. W.: Hyslop! (uttered in a tone of surprise) Oh, he says, Good; he's pleased.

E.G.: Lodge, this is terribly exhausting. I think you've got something now. Wait a bit, let Lodge think, and then let him speak and you rest. (To Lodge) Now you speak.

O.J.L.: I gather that you have been trying to explain, or rather illustrate the process of telepathy to me.

E.G.: Yes.

O.J.L.: And that you got William James through, and then a word that perhaps she does not know, Hyslop. Does she know it?

E.G.: Oh yes, she's read it, but she doesn't know why I say it, nor do you, in that juxtaposition. Let me know when the meaning that is there is seen by you. There may be a little time to pass first, but when the meaning is plain, say so.

O.J.L.: About telepathy, you mean it has to be purposed, that the thought cannot be picked up from stray people, that it has to be injected?

[1] *Proc.* S.P.R., Vol. xliii, pp. 237-8.
[2] 'Daylight Impression' see p. 20 above.

E.G.: What you say about telepathy isn't altogether right. It's not one thing and one process, but there are degrees of it, and it depends on the instrument partly and upon the familiarity of the agent. There must be practice on both sides.

Here's what appears to be a complete contradiction of what I've said, and yet both are facts. Through my carelessness she will sometimes see telepathically what I hadn't intended her to know. There are three more things that I can speak of. [Understood by O.J.L. to mean three processes of telepathy.]

There's the direct—directing—conscious—intended—what's the word?

O.J.L.: Impact?

E.G.: No, no, that's the other end—propulsion.

O.J.L.: Yes, I see.

Mrs. W.: The starting end he's speaking of.

O.J.L.: Yes;—emission? radiation?

E.G.: No, that's not the word I want, there's too many connotations about that. The sparking end—something like that—like two big clouds coming together and then the lightning; something like that. That's one kind; and then the other kind that led to this theory of unconscious mentality in the discarnate—the coma business, dream business. I can only talk, about it, say, pull out the stops I see in front of me. I'm putting it the way I can get it through.

Mrs. W.: He's encouraging me.

E.G.: I wish Lodge would tell you so.

O.J.L.: Yes, you are doing well.

E.G.: My [word illegible in notes] way of putting it is letting down a shutter. If I am what you would call very "close" to her, I could shut off certain impressions and then I can switch them on.

O.J.L.: Is it like removing a screen?

E.G.: Ah (he says), screen. Do you remember about a screen long ago? [Did not wait for an answer but continued] A third thing may happen;—when the shutter is down there may be a *leak*, without deliberate switching,—a general as against a specialized impact may take place. Do I express it?

O.J.L.: Yes, that is quite clear.

E.G.: In my record there's a case in point, that Mrs. Verrall has, of a leak which called out corresponding thought in the mind which was the very last I would have desired to stimulate. . . .

The three kinds of telepathic communication here enumerated have this in common, that they imply voluntary action on the part of the communicator.[1]

Gurney is saying two things about telepathy. One is that it is *dynamic*—something forcefully projected from agent to percipient. The other is that it is not one simple process: there are 'degrees' of it. In a D.I. of March 5th, 1912, Gurney says something more about it:

G.W.B.: If I understand you rightly, you spoke in an earlier D.I. of telepathy, inspiration, and mutual selection, as being distinct processes, forming a descending chain. Is that correct?

Say again. 1. 2. 3.

(G.W.B. repeats question. *D.I. immediately follows*.)

. . . Telepathy, inspiration, mutual selection—He says they mark different stages of the soul's commerce, it sounds like. He says it's very difficult to get it clear, but it's best for me to get some rough definitions down. He says, Telepathy is the action of mind upon mind; not of brain upon brain, but of mind upon mind. And he says, there are as many varieties of telepathy as there are varieties of human beings. He says, Telepathy shades off into inspiration, and inspiration shades off into mutual selection. . . .[2]

According to Gurney, telepathy is not a thing that fits into a neat category as physical processes do. It is probably inexpressible in words. Gurney and the struggling Mrs. Willett together get something through about it; but it is evidently impossible to get a complete description through. Telepathy is apparently something

[1] *Proc.* S.P.R., Vol. xliii, pp. 186-8.   [2] *Proc.* S.P.R., Vol. xliii, p. 252.

that opens out and out and eludes the mind more and more the further we pursue it.

Incidentally, it is of interest to note that Mrs. Willett is *there*, in her own consciousness all the time. She does not disappear and give place to a 'control' as does the ordinary medium; and this fact may account for the unusual clarity of these communications.

Telaesthesia. Gurney draws a marked distinction between telepathy and what he calls 'telaesthesia'. In a D.I. of October 8th, 1911, he says:

> . . . telaesthesia is a bedrock truth, a power of acquiring knowledge direct without the intervention of discarnate mind.
>
> Oh he says, telepathy's one thing—that's thought communication: telaesthesia is knowledge, not thought, acquired by the subliminal when operating normally in the metetherial.
>
> Oh he says, Here comes in our work again. Oh he says, what I'm saying may be used to cut at the spiritualistic hypothesis, but it doesn't. Again, who selects what of the total of telaesthetically acquired knowledge shall externalise itself—shall blend itself with those elements received by direct telepathic impact?
>
> Oh he says, Supposing I take her into a room and I screen off any action of my own mind on hers: her subliminal with its useful copious pinch of the salt of Eve's curiosity takes stock of the contents of the room. Normal consciousness is later regained, and lying in the subliminal is knowledge of certain objects perceived, not as the result of the action of my mind, but as the result of telaesthetic faculty. Oh he says, Here come I on script intent. Here be arrows for my quiver. Who selects which of all these—Have patience with me, oh, Edmund, I am trying, oh, I'm such a great way away. Oh, Edmund,—Oh he says, Who applies the stimulus under which certain ideas—use that word, not what I wanted—emerge, blended, which upon study will be found to be relevant to the total aim of that particular piece of automatism?[1]

[1] *Proc.* S.P.R., Vol. xliii, p. 194.

We gather from this that, speaking very roughly, telepathy is the deliberate projection of thought from one mind to another while telaesthesia is a kind of outward feeling of the mind in an attempt to draw knowledge into itself. Gurney distinguishes between thought and knowledge; and that is a distinction we cannot easily understand. He uses the analogy of a room into which the subliminal of Mrs. Willett goes and takes hold of what is there. One gathers that what is taken in is something between ideas and sense-imagery—something between thought and dream-scenery.

Another factor in the passage of mental material from the discarnate to the incarnate is what Gurney calls 'excursus'.

Success in the production of these scripts requires (we are told), on the part of the sensitive, 'a capacity for *Excursus* allied to a capacity for definite selection'; and by 'excursus' is meant a passing, as it were, outside herself and an entry into communion with the spiritual world. The communicator and the sensitive are represented as 'mutually selecting' from each other's minds —the communicator from the contents of 'the conscious and unconscious self' of the sensitive; the sensitive from 'such part of the mind of the communicating spirit as she can have access to.'

Under the heading of Mutual Selection comes the description of the rather elaborate process of choosing, guiding and shepherding to the point of emergence the topics which it is desired that the automatist should bring out. The subject is one of great interest, because it is not likely that Mrs. Willett, from her own reading or ideas on the subject, could have conceived the complexity of the process as Gurney describes it; or the wider, 'non-crystallised'[1] type of thought which is stated to exist in the deeper ranges of the self.

Somewhere in the depths of the self, the automatist has the power of *Excursus*, that is the power of passing 'as it were, outside herself and entering into communion with the spiritual world'. By means of this faculty of Excursus, the sensitive can select

[1] See pp. 31, 33 below.

material from 'such part of the mind of the communicating spirit as she can have access to'. This is the part which 'can naturally link onto human incarnate thought', and it includes the 'potential' as well as the 'actual' content of this mind.

The communicator is then able to exercise his selection on the material thus lying in the mind of the sensitive and to shepherd it upwards through the levels of the automatist's self towards emergence. That is what is meant by 'mutual selection'.

Gurney gives a concrete example of the way in which he selects from the minds of the sensitive or automatic writer with whom he is working:

> Say I wrote of horses. I get telepathically the idea of sound, clatter of the horses' gallop. I get the idea in a Verrall channel, for instance, of Pegasus; I get the idea, perhaps, of chariot races —equus, or something like that, he says—and I select and push up into its place where it will be grasped and externalised, two trump cards telaesthetically acquired—call it horseshoe, or, he says, the steeds of Dawn. The point is, I didn't place them there; I found and selected them: and the eight other elements—or objects—seen in the room remain dormant and never externalise themselves perhaps. The spiritualistic agency decides what element appropriate to its own activity shall emerge alongside and intertwined with matter placed in position by direct telepathic impact.[1]

Gurney says more about the 'room' in another script dated January 21st, 1912. It is an important description though not altogether easy to understand.

> (G.W.B. You referred at a former sitting to telaesthesia as a process by which the mind of the sensitive acquired knowledge on its own account. The subject came up in connection with what you call mutual selection. You spoke of taking the sensitive into a 'room' and screening off any action of your own mind on hers; whereupon her subliminal proceeds to take

[1] *Proc.* S.P.R., Vol. xliii, pp. 194-5.

stock of the contents of the room. Do you mean a real room, or only a room existing in your mind?)

I'll throw something at you, and you must make what you can of it.

I'll take that portion of her which can emerge in uprush, and I, as it were, link it on with that deeper subliminal standpoint, which can be in touch with what I want to get known; so that there is that portion of her which can normally acquire telaesthetically in its own deep profound plane passing on the knowledge to that plane from which an uprush can come.

Oh, he says, what I'm going to say to you now makes Sidgwick tear his hair because it's meaning the ocean in a child's bucket.

I'm going to call that deepest portion, nearer to the transcendental self—I'm going to call it—anything you like, any symbol, say H. Well, the H-self and I agree on what we want —what I want—to get transmitted, and which the H-self normally, in its own H-ness, through its own cognitive faculties can know. And here is the 'bucket' process, it's here where just because it's the most difficult I shall fail worst in trying to get near the thought. The H-self will touch the uprushable self just the grade below the uprushable, and the uprushable and the grade below will receive the knowledge from the H. But in putting it into the uprushable focus, as it were, it will know that a sort of crystallisation, often through symbolism, must be arrived at: and we will imagine, if we like, that having been foreseen both by me and the H-self, we determined upon what sort of crystals to aim at, so that the uprushable self has, as it were, presented to it what I called a 'room', the knowledge which the H-self is informing to the point where it becomes uprushable. Just below that uprushable point there's a sort of dim moment where both modes enter into cognition—I mean, where a knowledge of the thing as it is in the H-stage is united to a knowledge of the crystals which, the emblem which, can best express that which in its H-ness cannot, or rarely, uprush —for all these states are variable and the success variable. Then comes that moment of binding when the self that lies in juxtaposition to the uprushable absorbs the knowledge from H, and passes it on to the uprushable point in such a state as makes uprush possible. It then rushes out as words spoken or written, or dreams, or never-to-be-denied moments of prescience, precognition of supernormal knowledge. But that supernormal will contain within it the normally acquired knowledge of H— that element of normality will be there. Oh, he says, that isn't the invariable method, only one of them; and he says, The telepathic impact is another. . . .[1]

Although Gurney has done his best to explain the regions of the self behind normal consciousness and the processes which go on there when the dead are trying to communicate with the living, it is not altogether easy to follow him. I think it would be unreasonable to expect it to be easy. Lord Balfour paraphrases Gurney's description as follows: 'In answer to my question about the "room" Gurney distinguishes between different grades of the subliminal self. There is a deeper self which can telaesthetically acquire knowledge direct from the communicating spirit of that which he wants to get known. There is another self on a less profound plane to which the knowledge so acquired can be passed on, and through whose action it can emerge in *uprush*. There is also a self—"the self in juxtaposition to the uprushable"— which is intermediate between the other two. Let H stand for the deeper self; H_1 for the intermediate self; and H_2 for the self which is immediately responsible for the emergence of the message in written or spoken words. The communicator and H agree upon what they want to get transmitted, H having acquired knowledge of this through the faculty of telaesthetic cognition which is native to it in virtue of its H-ness. What happens next is admittedly difficult to explain, but it is something of this kind. Contact is effected in the first place between H and H_1, and later, through the mediation of H_1, between H and H_2. The knowledge which H has acquired from the communicator is thus passed on to both H_1 and H_2, but not in the form in which it has been acquired by H. In that form it would be all but impossible for it to emerge. Some change must take place analogous to crystallisation out of a state of fluidity. The individual crystals should be symbolic or emblematic of the knowledge acquired by H, but they are not the direct expression of that knowledge. Now it is possible for the necessary crystallisation to be brought about by concerted action between the communicator and H. They can decide what type of "crystals" are appropriate in the particular case. The crystallisation itself is effected in H_1, with the result that H_2 has presented to it what had been called a "room"—that is to say, a collection of "crystals" of a kind best fitted to express the knowledge acquired by H in a form in which it can be externalised. There is a dim moment when the original knowledge and its crystallised expression both enter into cognition together.

Finally comes the "binding", when, under the influence of the communicator, H, H_1, and H_2 are linked with one another. H_1 absorbs the knowledge from H and passes it on to H_2 in crystallised form. It is then automatically externalised, and may convey veridical messages, supernormal from the standpoint of the supraliminal self but embodying knowledge normally acquired by H through the exercise of its telaesthetic faculty.

'This is only one among several methods; direct telepathic emission is another.'[1]

What are we to gather from this explanation? The complex process of passing ideas through a sensitive—these different kinds of telepathy, the indefinable faculty of telaesthesia, the curious process of 'excursus', the limitations imposed on what can be selected, the necessity for 'crystallising' ideas into restricted forms which can be put into words, the chancy factor of what may or may not get through in 'uprush'—all these show that, if Gurney is speaking the truth, communication with a world outside this one is a highly complex matter, hazardous in the extreme and very severely limited. All has to pass in the end through a narrow bottle-neck. Gurney's descriptions do at any rate present the problem in perspective, and this gives them a sense of reality. It is not just a further extension of this world

[1] *Proc.* S.P.R., Vol. xliii, pp. 244-5.

which his words disclose: it is a step towards something far greater transcending our comprehension. According to Gurney, the self —or the H-selves—stretch far away beyond our normal consciousness in this world to uncomprehended modes of thought; and the way in which he transmits ideas through Mrs. Willett bears a comparison with the way in which intuitional and inspirational ideas come through into the consciousness of all thinkers. We know that inspirational influx is a fact and that the most valuable ideas do come in this way. Genius is founded on what comes through from beyond. Gurney's description, therefore, with its far-reaching implications, bears the stamp of truth.

But the most difficult problem is the status of the communicator. If we take different grades of communications and compare them with one another, it becomes obvious that another factor enters in, to which Gurney has not referred. In mediumistic communications of a low grade, the communicators are quite unconvincing. Their light patter evidently arises from some factor in the mind of the medium; but here again the solution may not be simple. On the next higher grade communicators become more characteristic of what they were in life and they remember significant incidents in their lives. The sitter has at times a feeling that the genuine communicator is there. This suggests a possibility. May it not be that when the difficult process of getting ideas through fails, a pseudo-personality or effigy is formed somewhere in the foreground and patters along unconvincingly, though claiming all the time to be the communicator? When conditions improve, the genuine communicator in the background might succeed in deflecting this run of patter towards the kind of things he wants to say. At a still higher grade the genuine communicator gains more control and the communications become clearer. Even in the present case, freedom and fluency are to some extent curbed by Mrs. Willett's difficulties over words and phrases and the obvious limitations she finds in trying to convey Gurney's explanations.

The question of whether the communicators are the deceased persons they claim to be is still one of difficulty: but the alternative view that they are pseudo-personalities constructed in the sensitive's unconscious raises far greater difficulties. On the latter view the histrionic qualities of Mrs. Willett's scripts would have to be attributed to her own 'unconscious'. All her stumbling efforts to keep up with Gurney would have to be regarded as a feat of play-acting. This is a tall order; and it is not all. Some of the ideas which the communicators endeavour to transmit are obviously beyond her. This comes out clearly in certain scripts which discuss which type of philosophy is most suitable to the mind-brain relation. In trying to transmit this, poor Mrs. Willett was almost overcome. And then we must remember the cross-correspondences, in which Mrs. Willett played a leading role.[1] These were broken up into fragments by the communicator and distributed among the automatists; and it was clearly stated that this was done deliberately in order to prove that a single mind had planned the whole and that they were not due to cross-telepathy among the automatists. The themes of the cross-correspondences were also based upon an erudite knowledge of the classics, which Mrs. Willett did not possess, but Myers, Gurney, A. W. Verrall, H. Butcher, who claim to have produced them, had all been first class classical scholars. It is true that Mrs. Verrall, who was one of the automatists, was also a first class classical scholar; and some thought that the classical cross-correspondences originated in her subconscious mind. But after her death, the classical themes continued, and no other living member of the group could have supplied them.

If we weigh the whole situation with as little bias as we can command, the facts point to the view that no communications of this kind are in the least like communications that take place in this world. They contain all kinds of complications; they involve an extension of the self which carries us beyond our ken; and the best communications are stamped with the characteristic personalities of the dead, reaching through from the background. The Willett communications make it abundantly clear why it is that no communicator can give a description of his life or of the world he is in, or send through items of profound wisdom or truth

[1] See *The Personality of Man*, chapter xvii.

beyond that which we can grasp in our present world. Everything that comes through has to run the gauntlet of all kinds of loss and distortion, and has finally to pass through a bottle-neck after being reduced to language that can express only things in our world and does not transcend what is familiar to the medium's mind.

There is another thing about the Gurney communications which gives rise to reflection. Gurney, and also Myers and the other communicators through Mrs. Willett, appear to be as natural and mundane as they were in the flesh. Gurney has the same humorous optimism that he had in life. Sidgwick is afraid that by the time the messages get through they will be distorted and misunderstood. Gurney's attempts to describe how messages originate in the larger and remoter part of Mrs. Willett's subliminal self makes Sidgwick 'tear his hair'. It seems to him like trying to pour the ocean into a bucket. This type of anxiety was characteristic of Sidgwick in life.

How is it that, having passed into the larger world Gurney Myers, Sidgwick and the rest are still so like what they were in life? But when we reflect, the answer occurs to us that perhaps they are not. Having entered into a larger and different world, they may also have entered into larger and different phases of selfhood, which match that world. Perhaps because they have to pass through the same narrowing and specialized channels that the messages themselves have to traverse, they may become temporarily narrowed and 'crystallized' too. Like the messages, they may be reduced to this-worldly forms of themselves—in fact to what they were when they lived in this world.

The chief value of this evidence seems to be that it opens up a new perspective. It does not tell us what the future life is or what we shall be like in it. It merely shows us that reality is there, opening out and leaving behind our little minds with their mundane thoughts. It is like the ocean seen from a point on the sea-shore. It is as though a voice said to us: There; now you can catch a glimpse of yourself and of the absurd, conceited folly that makes you think now that you can grasp everything there is. Now you have a chance of realizing that your little mind is adapted to grasp only a tiny corner of the universe. And even that corner you understand only in a pragmatic manner.

The sense of improbability when we transcend this material world is due in essence to the fact that our minds are so closely adapted to it. This makes matter appear to us to be the central thing in the universe and to be the originator of everything, and time, as we know it, to be universal, and life in time to be the only kind of life possible. We cannot believe that *being*, which shows itself throughout the graded order of all the world of life, and in the unseen properties of matter as well, has its origin in the roots of the universe. 'Being' appears only as tiny specks in the vastness of space: how can it be the central thing? For, as we say this, we assume that the spatial world is the centre. That the whole physical universe, so busily explored by the astronomer, and revealing dimensions so vast that they make the mind reel— that this physical universe is itself only an outlying suburb of reality, a sort of desert on the fringe of civilization—is a conception our minds refuse to entertain despite the facts that point towards it. They refuse because they are adapted to that desert world. Once this has been grasped, we shall be on our guard for unconscious assumptions which lead our thinking to foregone conclusions. Our belief to-day that the physical universe occupies the centre, indeed the whole, of reality arises from the same mental fixation which caused our ancestors to assume that the earth was the centre of the universe and that the sun, moon and stars were attendants which circle round it. Discovered facts are accepted; but it is nevertheless true that the shape of our outlook is there from the start and we tend to manipulate evidence to make it fit into our outlook. The advance of science is bringing this situation gradually to light, but so far it has modified the character of our minds to a very small extent.

If being or selfhood, and not matter, is primary in the universe, our existence outside the space-time world is not at all improbable: but here the fixed character of our mind comes in and insists that the material world to which it is adapted is the centre. The mind, too, is without perspective and regards anything unfamiliar as an absurdity. Are we, for example,

basically separated as individuals and always bound to remain so;
or shall we ultimately merge into a conglomerate human mass?
The adapted mind will never see that *both* these ideas belong to
the material world which is its province, and that beyond that
world, in the range of being or selfhood, neither need be true.
The logic of this world can be transcended and reality soon passes
beyond our reach. Besides, how far does our knowledge even of
this world go? What is matter? Can we answer this question
comprehensively? What is the ultimate character of the brain
with which the practical level of our consciousness is so closely
integrated? How do we know that it does not possess properties
in the background which our senses do not reveal and which may
be very different from the properties with which we are familiar?
These background properties might differ very much from the
foreground properties which are of a spatial kind and are the only
type of property which our senses allow us to investigate. There,
in the background, may exist the essential relations between brain
and mind; and that would supply a reason for the fact that mind
does not stand out as an isolable entity in the sense-field in the way
which science demands that it must do unless it is merely a
function of matter as we know it through our senses.

This possibility that both mind and matter extend beyond our
this-world purview is not pure speculation. The evidence of
psychical research supports it; so too does the lay-out of the
universe as far as we have explored it, for it is highly improbable
that it comes to an end where our senses reach their limits.
Before attempting to assess the evidence for a future life, it
is therefore necessary in the first place to realize something
of our own situation, our specialized mentality and the limitations
and coercive forces under which we live and think. The pragmatic
tendencies within us may falsify our whole outlook unless we are
aware of them.

Many years ago, the philosopher William James pointed out
that there are three possible types of relation between mind and
brain—productive, transmissive and permissive.[1] The productive
type of relation seems obvious to our minds because we place

---

[1] *Human Immortality*, Ingersoll Lectures for 1897-8, p. 25.

matter at the centre of things. But the evidence for telepathy and
extra-sensory perception does not point to it, for the arguments
against a physical theory of telepathy are overwhelming; and
precognition is quite incompatible with the view that physical
traces in the brain cause knowledge of the future. Never mind,
whispers the adapted self; the productive theory *must* hold the
field: the evidence for telepathy and precognition can easily be
ignored! It is this coercive tendency to reach a foregone conclusion that causes us to regard the normally conscious self of
everyday life as the whole of our being, although intuition,
inspiration, the paranormal and religion all point in the opposite
direction. Even psychologists are prone to adopt this view in
spite of the fact that psychology itself, in its modern develop-
ments, points against it.

Gurney's accounts of communications, if we accept it, gives a
most instructive glimpse of the greater self beyond normal consciousness. We cannot comprehend what goes on in these ever-
widening fields. Communications of good quality such as these
strongly suggest that the dead are working behind the scenes,
doing what they can to shepherd certain ideas, with varying
degrees of success, through paths strewn with great psychological
obstacles. But the point of chief importance for us to grasp is that
these difficulties are not likely to be reduced to complete com-
prehensibility by ourselves; for the more they are pursued the
further they recede into the unknown.

Mediumistic communications, regarded as a whole, dispel the
surface view that a direct and simple exchange of messages takes
place on the lines of communications in this world, which is the
usual view in spiritualistic circles. At the same time they dispel the
theory that the problem can be solved by postulating a temporary
pseudo-personality in the medium's unconscious, although
something of this kind may be a factor in lower-grade communications. No pat and ready answer accords with the facts,
though it does respond to the tendency of our own minds. The
Gurney explanation suggests something far more in line with the
modern outlook, for it suggests a vista within ourselves, stretching
away into the unknown and passing beyond our comprehension.

4

From this far territory it would seem that the dead can communicate when the conditions are favourable; but what comes through if it has escaped distortion, must be reduced to our own limited way of thinking before we can receive it.

The chief thing to realize is that the best evidence throws the question into a far-reaching perspective. How much of it do we grasp? How much of the view we tend to take is supplied by the specialized characteristics of our own minds? How much is the wide-spread assumption that the dead no longer exist due to the pragmatic character of our thinking? It is our *own* minds which need to be subjected to careful scrutiny if we are to make any valid advance in knowledge beyond the everyday world.

CHAPTER IV

The Light thrown by Apparitions

AN interesting branch of psychical research, which was not dealt with in *The Personality of Man*, is that concerned with accounts of apparitions. The Society for Psychical Research has accumulated a large number of such cases, and, like all work done by that body, they rest on sound evidence.

Soon after it was founded, the Society went into the question of sensory appearances very thoroughly by carrying out a Census of Hallucinations. A question was drafted, which read as follows : 'Have you ever, when believing yourself to be completely awake, had a vivid impression of seeing or being touched by a living being or inanimate object, or of hearing a voice; which impression so far as you could discover, was not due to any external physical cause?' The three senses of sight, hearing and touch were therefore included. This question was circulated to 17,000 persons, of whom 15,316 replied No, and 1684 replied Yes. This meant that nearly 10 per cent. of those questioned stated that they had had sensory hallucinations.

Those who answered Yes were asked to give detailed reports of their experiences, which were carefully examined and classified. The collectors were on the look-out for the following possible sources of error: (1) Inaccuracies in the narratives. This is a matter to be decided by individual judgement after each case has been studied separately. (2) The possibility that the collectors may have selected death-cases by going to persons they knew had had them. It is shown that at any rate in many of the cases the collectors knew nothing about the percipients' previous experiences before issuing the Census Question. (3) The possibility that expectation, or some other normal cause, may account for the coincidence. This was carefully considered and more than sufficient weight seems to have been attached to it.

41

After this census, a steady flow of cases came in, covering a period of many years. The collectors were critical and asked: (1) Is the account first hand? (2) Was it written before the event? (3) Has the witness been corroborated? (4) Was the percipient awake at the time? (5) Was the percipient educated and of good character? (6) Was the apparition recognized? (7) Was it seen out of doors? (8) Was the percipient in a state of anxiety or expectancy? (9) Could details have been put back into the narrative after the event? (10) If the experience coincided with an actual event of the same kind, could the coincidence be due to chance? The cases collected were therefore far above the level of hearsay evidence.

Expectancy is often cited as the cause of coincidence between a dream or waking apparition and the occurrence of a similar event in real life ; and this possibility has certainly to be allowed for. But it is easy to overestimate its explanatory power, as the following example shows. The friend of a certain lady was so ill that his death was expected at any time. The lady had a dream, in which she saw a corpse laid out on a bed; but it was not the corpse of her male friend, who was so ill, but the corpse of his wife. So far as she knew, the wife was not ill at all; but news arrived saying that she had been suddenly taken ill, and shortly afterwards she died. Thus knowledge from a paranormal source was not deflected by expectation.

As the apparitional cases accumulated, it was found that they fell into four main classes : (1) 'On Friday December 1st, 1882, at 9.30 p.m., I went into a room alone and sat by the fireside, and endeavoured so strongly to fix my mind upon the interior of a house at Kew, in which resided Miss V. and her two sisters, that I seemed to be actually in the house. During this experience I must have fallen into a mesmeric sleep, for although I was conscious, I could not move my limbs. I did not seem to have lost the power of moving them, but I could not make the effort to do so, and my hands, which lay loosely on my knees, about six inches apart, felt involuntarily drawn together and seemed to meet although I was conscious that they did not move.

'At 10 p.m. I regained my normal state by an effort of the will, and then took a pencil and wrote down on a sheet of note-paper the foregoing statements.

'When I went to bed on the same night, I determined that I would be in the front bedroom of the above-mentioned house at 12 p.m., and remain there until I had made my spiritual presence perceptible to the inmates of that room.

'On the next day, Saturday, I went to Kew to spend the evening, and met there a married sister of Miss V. (namely Mrs. L.)'

The narrator had only met this lady once before. 'In the course of conversation', he continues, '(although I did not think for a moment of asking her any questions on such a subject), she told me that on the previous night she had seen me distinctly on two occasions. She had spent the night at Clarence Road and had slept in the front bedroom. At about half-past nine she had seen me in the passage going from one room to another, and at 12 p.m. when she was wide awake, she had seen me enter the bedroom and walk round to where she was sleeping, and take her hair (which is very long) into my hand. She also told me that the apparition took hold of her hand, and gazed intently into it, whereupon she spoke saying, 'You need not look at the lines, for I have never had any trouble'. She then awoke her sister, Miss V., who was sleeping with her and told her about it. After hearing this account, I took the statement, which I had written down on the previous evening, from my pocket, and showed it to some of the persons present, who were much astonished, although incredulous. I asked Mrs. L. if she was not dreaming at the time of the latter experience, but this she stoutly denied, and stated that she had forgotten what I was like, but seeing me so distinctly she recognized me at once.'

The lady and her sister give a corroboration. Intense concentration by the agent before going to sleep is mentioned in other cases of this kind.

Two features to be noticed about this case are: (1) the agent's figure is seen walking down the passage very much as a figure is often seen in cases of haunting, and (2) the agent's figure approaches the percipient's bed and behaves with apparent consciousness of her, very much as a crisis-apparition behaves.

The similarity between this experimental case and the spontaneous cases discussed below is obvious. I have found records of sixteen occasions on which this experiment has been tried with success, and in most cases success has been achieved on the first attempt. Here then, is a repeatable experiment which for some reason or other appears to have been ignored by investigators. It is clearly an important experiment, for if it could be repeated at will, it would be known when and where to expect such apparitions, and one could be prepared with the means for testing them —with cameras, sound-recording apparatus or the like. Moreover, the states of the agent could be studied; hypnosis and suggestion could be applied and so on. On several of the recorded occasions the agent, after concentrating his mind strongly on the selected percipient (who was ignorant that any experiment was being tried), went to sleep; and it was while he was asleep that the apparition was seen.

Mr. J. Kirk [1] made nine successful experiments (only one of which has been counted in the above sixteen, because on only one occasion was his apparition actually seen) and these are of great interest, because they bridge the gap between experimental apparitions and experimental telepathy. For example, in one experiment Mr. Kirk, instead of trying to make his own apparition seen, tried to make the percipient see a bright disc at which he was looking. She saw luminous clouds which concentrated into a disc.

There are many examples of Crisis Cases which happened a long time ago. Here is a brief account of a more recent one.[2] It occurred to Mrs. Dick-Cunyngham, and was brought to notice through the good offices of Mr. Douglas Fawcett.

The vision seen was of Mr. Eustace Neville Craig, a close friend of Mrs. Dick-Cunyngham. The latter, writing to Mr. Fawcett recently, said in reference to her experience : 'I did not even know he had been suddenly taken ill (operation). One Sunday I had gone to church in London with my mother. Suddenly I got the clearest vision I have ever seen. It was like a shutter opened slowly and then closed again slowly. For two

---

[1] *Journal* S.P.R., Vol. v, pp. 21-30.
[2] *Journal* S.P.R., Sept.-Oct., 1944, pp. 72-4.

seconds I saw Eustace lying quite motionless on a bed, his eyes were closed, he was as white as a sheet. There were two nurses in white caps; one was advancing holding a glass of medicine. Then the vision vanished. I came home and said to Dixon (her maid), "I believe Mr. Craig is ill". The following Tuesday his death was in *The Times*. Afterwards I heard he had never recovered consciousness after an operation.'

In reply to a request for further details, Mrs. Dick-Cunyingham wrote: '. . . Unfortunately it [the incident] took place a long while ago in May 1932. . . . Though so long ago I remember it as if it had occurred yesterday. The "vision" came to me during morning service (during the prayers after the first hymn) at the church of St. Paul's, Knightsbridge. It seemed to me as if I suddenly saw a *spot* of light, round in shape. This enlarged rather slowly. Then I saw the picture I described inside the circle only for a second. Then, as if curtains were drawn over it, very slowly it faded. No, I had no special reason for thinking of Eustace Craig at that moment, except that I had not heard anything from him or of him for some time, which was unusual, as we were very great friends, and I did not know he was ill. I mentioned the incident to my maid (who has been with me about twenty years) because she is, I think, genuinely psychic. Yes, she remembers about it, and would corroborate. . . . The exact date (offhand) I cannot remember. I believe it may have been May 14 or 18, but I know it was May 1932. The vision was on *Sunday*. Notice of death, Eustace Neville Craig, in *The Times* two days later, Tuesday. . . . Some weeks after Eustace died I had another vision of him (not so strong). I saw him quite plainly standing at the end of my bed. He did not speak. I have had talks with him through a medium several times. . . . He himself was not interested in psychic things. No, I do not very often have "visions"; that is why I said it was the "clearest vision I had ever had", but I very often seem to know things that are going to happen. . . . Yours very truly, Vera Dick-Cunyngham.'

This case bears a striking similarity to the older cases in the Society's collection. The phrases, 'the clearest vision I have ever seen', and 'though so long ago I remember it as if it had occurred yesterday' echo almost verbally the comments of many bygone percipients with regard to the vividness and impressiveness of their experiences.

The vision possessed, also, two special features: (1) On the first occasion it appeared in a special space of its own. (2) It emerged out of a bright spot or cloud; but on the second occasion it appeared in physical space. There is a popular tendency to believe that an apparition which appears in physical space and takes its normal place among the surroundings, must be in some sense more objectively 'there' than an apparition which appears in a special space of its own, or appears in a dream. But the apparent indifference of apparitions to the kind of space they appear in would seem to negative this belief. The kind of spatial setting is surely merely part of the chosen dramatic form given to the figure: it is not evidence that an apparition is *actually* present when it appears in another kind of space. The present case falls exactly into line with previous cases in this respect.

Mrs. Dick-Cunyngham has kindly given permission for the real names and addresses to be printed.

The third group deals with apparitions of people long dead. Mrs. P.[1] and her husband had gone to bed, but she, wrapped in her dressing-gown, was lying on the outside of the bed, waiting to attend to her baby, which lay in a cot beside her. The lamp was still alight and the door of the room was locked. She says, 'I was just pulling myself into a half sitting posture against the pillows, thinking of nothing but the arrangements for the following day, when, to my great astonishment I saw a gentleman standing at the foot of the bed, dressed as a naval officer, and with a cap on his head having a projecting peak. The light being in the position which I have indicated, the face was in shadow *to me*, and the more so that the visitor was leaning upon his arms which rested on the foot rail of the bedstead. I was too astonished to be afraid, but simply wondered who it could be; and instantly touching my husband's shoulder (whose face was turned from me), I said, "Willie, who is this?" My husband turned, and, for a second or two, lay looking in intense astonishment at the intruder; then,

[1] *Proc.* S.P.R., Vol. viii, p. 26.

lifting himself a little, he shouted, "What on earth are you doing here, sir?" Meanwhile the form, slowly drawing himself into an upright position, now said, in a commanding yet reproachful voice, "Willie, Willie". I looked at my husband and saw that his face was white and agitated. As I turned towards him he sprang out of bed as though to attack the man, but stood by the bedside as if afraid, or in great perplexity, while the figure calmly and slowly moved *towards the wall* at right angles with the lamp in the direction of the dotted line. (A diagram is included with the account.) As it passed the lamp, a deep shadow fell upon the room as of a material person shutting out the light from us by his intervening body, and he disappeared, as it were, into the wall. My husband now, in a very agitated manner, caught up the lamp and turning to me, said, "I mean to look all over the house to see where he has gone", I was by this time exceedingly agitated too, but, remembering that the door was locked, and that the mysterious visitor had not gone towards it at all, remarked, "He has not gone out by the door". But without pausing, my husband *unlocked* the door, hastened out of the room, and was soon searching the whole house.'

Mrs. P. was wondering if the apparition could indicate that her brother, who was in the navy, was in some trouble, when her husband came back and exclaimed, ' "Oh no, it was my father". *My husband's father had been dead fourteen years:* he had been a naval officer in his young life.'

During the following weeks Mr. P. became very ill and then disclosed to his wife that he had got into financial difficulties and, at the time of the apparition, was inclined to take advice of a man who would probably have ruined him.

Here, again, the figure is life-like and intrudes on the percipients suddenly and unexpectedly. There is in fact no intrinsic difference between it and a crisis-apparition.

The fourth class is that of ghosts which haunt houses. The following example is old but was at the time extremely well authenticated. Miss R. C. Morton[1] (pseudonym) a medical student, evidently had, from the way she reports her researches, a

[1] *Proc.* S.P.R., Vol. viii, pp. 311-29.

well-balanced, scientific mind and was free from superstitious fears. She, as well as the principal observers in the case, were personally interviewed by Frederic Myers. The following points should be noted.

(1) The hauntings lasted for seven years from 1882 to 1889.

(2) During this period about twenty people heard the ghost and of these at least seven saw it; probably more.

(3) The hauntings rose to a peak period in 1885, and after 1886 gradually faded away.

(4) The figure was usually taken for a real person by those who saw it for the first time.

(5) All the observers agreed as to the description of the figure, which was tall, wearing a dark dress with widow's weeds, one hand usually half hidden in the folds and a handkerchief held to the face. One observer did not see the handkerchief. The face was never well seen, but the general description tallied with the appearance and habits of Mrs. S., the second wife of a former tenant.

(6) The house dated from about 1860 and had only been occupied by two families before the Morton family, and their history was known.

(7) The phenomena consisted of the visual apparition, which followed, more or less, a routine going down the stairs from the bedroom landing to the drawing-room, standing at a particular spot in the bow-window, then leaving the drawing-room by the door, going along the passage and disappearing by the garden door.   Also footsteps were heard by many percipients, always of the same description. 'Her footstep is very light', says Miss Morton, 'you can hardly hear it except on the linoleum, and then only like a person walking softly with thin boots on.'   The swish of woollen drapery was also heard. These footsteps were unlike any of those of the Morton family. All the servants were changed during the period of hauntings; but the footsteps went on unaltered. There were other sounds, especially during the peak period, of bumps, turning of door handles, heavy and irregular footsteps, heavy thuds and bumpings, noises like heavy articles, such as boots, being thrown across the passage, and the sound of something heavy being dragged.

(8) The sounds were sometimes collectively perceived, as many as five persons having heard them at once. The visual apparition never seems to have been actually seen by more than one person at a time; but it was on one occasion seen by the four Miss Mortons in quick succession in four consecutive positions on its route from the drawing-room to the orchard.

(9) Besides the evidence of awareness of its situation provided by the behaviour of the figure in walking up and down stairs, through doorways and along passages, etc. (Miss Morton once saw the figure deliberately walk round her father, who could not see it) on more than one occasion it stopped and looked as if about to speak when Miss Morton addressed it.

(10) The non-physical character of the figure was proved in several ways. It appeared in a room with the doors shut; it vanished while being watched; it was twice seen to pass through threads lightly fastened across the stairs; it only became substantial and solid looking towards the end of the period. It was obvious that no *physical* sounds could be caused by the feet of a figure having no substantiality; for sound-waves are caused only by the reaction on one another of physical bodies. Miss Morton's frequent attempts to touch the figure failed because it always managed to place its visible surface beyond her reach. Sometimes one person would see the figure while another present would not. Miss Morton's father never saw it, although she pointed out to him the place where she saw it, and he went and stood by it. It then moved round him.

(11) The figure had no luminosity of its own and behaved with reference to the lighting of the scene as a material figure would have done.

(12) Cold feelings, or a cold wind, sometimes accompanied the figure.

(13) The dogs were affected by the apparition. A retriever was several times found in the kitchen in a state of terror. A Skye terrier twice ran to the foot of the stairs, wagging his tail at an invisible something, and jumping up and fawning. Then it suddenly slunk away with its tail between its legs and ran under a sofa.

(14) Miss Morton says, 'I felt conscious of a feeling of *loss* as if I had lost power to the figure'. Also some mental connection between the figure and the percipients is indicated by the fact that 'the figure has not been called up by desire to see it, for on every occasion when we had made special arrangements to watch for it, we never saw it.   On several occasions we have sat up at night hoping to see it, but in vain—my father with my brother-in-law, myself and a friend three or four times, an aunt and myself twice, and my sisters with friends more than once; but on none of these occasions was anything seen. Nor have the appearances been seen after we have been talking or thinking much of the figure.'

All this shows that there is a large element of subjectivity in ghost-seeing. Whether or not the ghost is seen depends on the make-up of the observer and on the direction his thoughts are taking. But the whole thing is not subjective; for the fact that the ghost is seen only in one particular place indicates that there is an objective factor as well—and in this case the objective factor was clearly connected with a former inhabitant of the house.

Returning to crisis-apparitions, the question arises as to whether or not the relation between the subjective and objective features is due to chance.

When considering the possibility that the coincidence between the experience and the event may be due to chance, the following considerations must be taken into account.

'Coincidence' was defined by the collectors of the crisis cases as occurring only if the event happened within twelve hours before or after the experience. Even striking likenesses at greater intervals were not counted as coincidental cases.

Again, it has to be remembered that as a rule, neither the event nor the experience consists of one incident only. If a sequence of incidents in the experience coincided with a similar sequence of incidents in the event, the likelihood of chance-coincidence diminishes very rapidly.

The argument is frequently put forward that when the experience is a dream, because dreams are so many, the probability of chance coincidence is very large indeed. This argument may be valid in some cases; but it has to be remembered that not infrequently the dream-experience that coincides with the event differs considerably in character from an ordinary dream. Therefore to class it with ordinary dreams for statistical purposes is to introduce a methodological error. The following were included in some reports of cases: 'I rushed down to the drawing-room again, and, sinking on my knees by my husband's side, fainted and it was with difficulty I was restored to myself again.' Again the percipient burst into tears when asked about her experience and said, 'I suppose I fainted, as I lost all recollection for some time, and when I came to myself the apparition had gone—but one thing I am sure, and that is *that it was not a dream*. It made such an impression on my mind I shall never forget it.' 'The following circumstance is impressed upon my mind in a manner which will preclude its ever being forgotten by me or the members of the family interested.' 'It is nearly thirty years ago now, but it is as vividly impressed on her memory as if it had happened yesterday.' 'I only know I shall never forget it.' 'She was terribly frightened, rushed into a nieghbour's house and dropped in the passage.' 'I turned round and saw my husband's mother, looking very death-like. I said, "Oh mother, what a start you gave me!" But she was gone. A feeling of great depression came over me, and I was quite unable to go on my husband's errand, but went home. . . . I fainted before I saw Mr. Alger and after recovering, I felt unwell so that I had to go to bed.' People do not behave like this every time they have a dream.

A study of well evidenced cases of apparitions seen when the percipient was awake shows that they possess the following characteristics:

(1) They do not always appear in physical space, looking like material objects. They sometimes appear in a space of their own. The wall may seem to open and the apparition appear in it; or a face may appear as if reflected in a polished piece of furniture.

(2) The great majority of the cases that have been carefully collected point to their subjective character. The apparitions may appear and disappear in locked rooms: they often vanish while being watched: they may become transparent and fade away: they

are frequently seen and heard only by some of the persons present, which seems to indicate that they are not reflecting physical light, or creating physical sound: they disappear into walls or closed doors and can pass through physical objects: people have put their hands through them and have walked through them without encountering any resistance: they leave no physical traces behind them.

It is true there are some cases of apparitions which give evidence of being genuinely physical; for some have been photographed and the type called 'poltergeists' move physical objects about. These may belong to a different class; for the great majority of apparitional cases collected by the Society for Psychical Research give every indication that they are subjective, that is to say, they are hallucinations of the senses. Of course such hallucinations need not originate entirely in the percipient. The cause of the hallucinations may be outside him. In the case of a ghost, for instance, which appears again and again and is recognized as a former occupant of the house, the appearance may be entirely subjective, yet the cause of it may possibly reside in the person depicted.

Another characteristic of apparitions when they appear in ordinary space is their remarkable likeness to persons in the flesh. Occasionally they have been known to react in their movements to the presence of those who are watching them. Another curious thing is that apparitions have been seen to cast shadows as they passed in front of lamps. This, however, is no proof of their objectivity; for the visual hallucination is minutely constructed to react to its surroundings.

Again, there are quite a number of cases in which an apparition has been seen collectively. So far as can be gathered from all those accounts, the two or three percipients see the apparition in the same place and looking, on the whole, the same. One example is given on page 63 of *The Personality of Man*.

A certain Canon Bourne and his two daughters were out hunting, and the daughters decided to return home with the coachman while their father went on. 'As we were turning to go home', say the two Misses Bourne in a joint account, 'we distinctly saw my father waving his hat to us and signing us to follow him. He was on the side of a small hill, and there was a dip between him and us. My sister, the coachman and myself all recognized my father and also the horse. The horse looked so dirty and shaken that the coachman remarked he thought there had been a nasty accident. As my father waved his hat I clearly saw the Lincoln and Bennett mark inside, though from the distance we were apart it ought to have been utterly impossible for me to have seen it. . . . Fearing an accident, we hurried down the hill. From the nature of the ground we had to lose sight of my father, but it took us a few seconds to reach the place where we had seen him. When we got there, there was no sign of him anywhere, nor could we see anyone in sight at all. We rode about for some time looking for him but could not see or hear anything of him. We all reached home within a quarter of an hour of each other. My father then told us he had never been in the field, nor near the field in which we thought we saw him, the whole of that day. He had never waved to us and had met with no accident. My father was riding the only white horse that was out that day.'[1]

One might quote also the much more recent case of the two holiday makers who both saw a guest-house with brightly coloured umbrellas on the lawn as they passed in a bus. When they went back to book rooms in it, it had vanished.[2] At first sight collective cases appear to be rare. When looking through the records of the Society for Psychical Research I found 130 cases; but there are probably more. This is not a large percentage on the whole; but the reason of this comes to light when one reads the cases carefully. It is that in the majority of cases in which apparitions are seen, the percipient is alone; there is no one present to share the experience. If one takes the number of cases in which more than one person is present, collective visual hallucination is not particularly rare.

Collective perception of an apparition does not involve the objectivity of the apparition; for our minds are interrelated beneath the conscious surface, as the ample evidence for telepathy

[1] *Journal* S.P.R., Vol. vi, p. 129.   [2] *The Personalty of Man*, p. 65.

has proved. But this, and the extraordinarily accurate assimilation of apparitions to external circumstances, such as dimness when the light fades, and the casting of a shadow, shows how subtle, and detailed these created hallucinations can be. They can be so exactly like material objects as to be indistinguishable from them. Yet on occasion, when there is some reason for it, apparitions can show vivid details when it is almost dark or at a normally impossible distance. The resemblance to the physical is therefore artificial.

Another important thing about these visual creations is that they can be very extensive. There is the case of Miss Ruth Wynne and her pupil, for example.[1] The two were out for a walk in 1926 near Bury St. Edmunds, and after passing through a farm-yard they came to a road flanked by a high brick wall. Following the wall they came to some tall wrought-iron gates, through which they could see the drive, leading to what was evidently a large house among trees. A corner of the house, with stucco front and Georgian windows, was visible. It was some months before they took the same walk again. Passing once more through the farm-yard, they came out upon the road: but there was no brick wall, no iron gates, no drive and no house. The road was flanked with a ditch, beyond which was tumbled earth, with mounds and a pond. No one in the neighbourhood had ever heard of the house they saw. The well-known experiences of Miss Moberley and Miss Jourdain in the gardens of Versailles is another example of this kind of wide-spread hallucination. Evidently visual hallucinations are not necessarily restricted to a single figure or object: they can provide whole surroundings. But they rarely do so; and the reason why they do not is plain. If sensory hallucinations were frequent and on a large scale, no one's life would be safe. We must see, hear and feel things as they are or we should soon be killed.

In March, 1938, an interesting experience happened to a Mr. J. S. Spence, who was taking a holiday in South Devon.[2]

---

[1] *Apparitions*, pp. 46-7, Myers Memorial Lecture, 1942, by G. N. M. Tyrrell, published by the Society for Psychical Research.
[2] *Journal* S.P.R., June-July, 1947.

He entered a cave in a headland, but had an unpleasant feeling of being watched; so he turned and came out again. But a feeling of depression came over him and he had the impression that something was straining at a leash. Climbing up the cliff by a little path, he found himself waist-deep in bracken and bramble. He came to a long wall, made without mortar, the stones of which looked fresh and were not covered with creeper. Looking at the ordnance map he had with him, he saw marked on it a gate and a solitary tree at the other side of the headland. But neither were there: only a few stunted trees bent by the wind. As he went on the atmosphere seemed to become less charged and less tense, and for the first time he heard a sound—a seagull screaming overhead. Then looking ahead, he saw the lone tree and the gate as marked on the map; and the grass was fresher and greener and there was less bracken.

Next day he set out to go to the cave again, and the tide was up far higher than it could have been in comparison with the day before. After it had gone down sufficiently, he found the place where he had entered the cave; but the entry was nearly blocked by rubble, and he decided not to try to enter. Climbing up the cliff he felt once more the atmosphere charged with strain and unfriendliness: the same tight feeling came across his forehead and he felt the sweat breaking out. Again the bracken became waist-deep. He followed the wall, made of neat slabs of stone until suddenly he felt giddy, though he could see the wall stretching away in front of him. On impulse, he took a snap with his camera of the view in front of him. Another pace, and his left foot slipped as if into a rabbit-hole. He collapsed onto his other foot and wildly seized two tufts of grass. For a moment everything went black: then he found himself on the edge of the cliff, clinging to the grass. He pulled himself to safety and made his way home. The photograph, when developed, looked straight down on to the sea-shore below. The wall had now changed and appeared very old, covered by brambles and partly in ruins.

This shows how dangerous large scale hallucinations would be, and why they so seldom occur. But when the mind is not on the *qui vive*, as it always is in daily life, sensory hallucinations can take

5

charge. Mrs.Willett, in the aloof state in which she could still speak and describe things, had a remarkably vivid vision of a scene taken from Plato's *Symposium*.[1] She said of the figures in the scene: 'I know them much better than many of the people I live with.' And also : 'Do you know that man's as real to me as if I could touch him!' Yet this picture was created only by the reading of an account of the scene in a book.

So it seems that if the safety device, which in waking life concentrates all attention on the deliveries of the sense-organs, lapses into abeyance, the mind can create environments which are just as real, to all appearance, and just as complete as those the senses provide.

When comparing the large number of cases of apparitions recorded in the *Proceedings* and *Journal* of the Society for Psychical Research, it is interesting to collect and bring together those characteristics. Very few apparitions possess individually all those characteristics, but the evidence for each of them is good, and it is instructive to endow an imaginary apparition with them all. Let us imagine, then, that a 'perfect apparition' of a human figure is standing beside an ordinary human being. There would be the following points of resemblance and of difference, each of which is taken from well evidenced cases collected by the Society for Psychical Research.

(1) Both figures would stand out in space and would appear equally real and solid. The apparition would be just as clear and vivid in matters of detail, such as the colour and texture of skin and clothing, as the material person.

(2) We should be able to walk round the apparition, viewing it from any distance and from any standpoint, and, as regards distance and perspective, we should detect no difference between it and the living person.

(3) If the light happened to be poor, both figures would be badly seen, and if more light were turned on, both figures would appear brighter. If the light went out, both figures would disappear in the darkness.

(4) Both figures would obscure the background.

[1] *The Personality of Man*, pp. 161-2.

(5) If the apparition happened to be wearing a rose in its button-hole, we would probably smell the scent of it.

(6) On approaching the apparition, we should hear it breathing and we should hear the rustle of its clothes as it moved and its shoes would shuffle on the floor.

(7) The apparition would probably behave as if aware of our presence, looking at us in a natural way and possibly smiling and turning its head to follow our movements. It might even place its hand on our shoulder, in which case we should feel an ordinary human touch.

(8) The apparition might speak to us, and possibly it might go as far as to answer a question; but we should not be able to engage it in any long conversation.

(9) If a mirror were fixed to the wall we should see the apparition reflected in it at the appropriate angle, just as we should see the reflection of the real man.

(10) Both figures would probably cast shadows, but the evidence on this point is uncertain.

(11) If we were to shut our eyes or turn our head, the apparition would disappear just as the figure by its side would do. And on reopening them, we should see it again.

(12) In addition to its clothes, the figure might have accessories such as a stick or any other object. And it might be accompanied by a dog or even by another human being. These would appear normal and behave in a normal manner. With regard to a human companion, I do not think it would make any difference whether he had ever existed or not. Mr. Pickwick or Sherlock Holmes would probably do as well as Charles Dickens or Sir Arthur Conan Doyle, and would appear just as alive and natural.

(13) The apparition might pick up any object in the room or open and close the door. We should both see and hear these objects moved: yet physically they would never have moved at all.

In these points the apparition's imitation of a material figure would be perfect. But we should find points of difference no less striking.

(14) For one thing, as soon as we came near the apparition, or if the apparition touched us, we might feel a sensation of cold.

(15) If we tried to take hold of the apparition, our hand would go through it without encountering any resistance. In the most perfect case I am not quite sure about this; for the sensation of touch is undoubtedly hallucinated in such cases, and it might be that we should *feel* our hand stopped at the surface of the apparition's body, as by something impenetrable; but at the same time we should *see* our hand go through it without let or hindrance. Apparitions when cornered avoid this interesting situation by disappearing.

(16) If we were to sprinkle French chalk on the floor and could induce the apparition and the human being to walk on it together, we should find that only the real man left any footprints, although we should hear the footsteps of both.

(17) If we were to take a photograph of the two figures, only the real man would come out. And if we had a sound-recording apparatus, only the sounds made by the real man would be recorded. It is true that these inferences do not rest on direct evidence. But the non-physical character of apparitions is so clear that the inference seems to be inescapable.

(18) After a time, which might be anything up to half an hour or so, the apparition would disappear. It might suddenly vanish; or it might become slightly transparent and fade away; it might vanish into the wall or go down through the floor; or it might, conventionally, open the door and walk out.

(19) Sometimes we should probably find that the apparition did not imitate the behaviour of the material man quite so closely. It might, for instance, become slightly luminous; it might show small details of itself when we were so far away from it that normally we could not possibly have seen them; it might even so far forget itself as to make us see it through the back of our head!

These points of resemblance and of difference between an apparition and a physical human being, which a careful examination of collected cases reveals, show how minutely regulated hallucinations of the senses can be. Perhaps 'sensory constructs' is a better term to use than 'sensory hallucinations'; for such cases make it plain that perception of an entire environment, as complete in every way as that which surrounds us in daily life, can be constructed by the mind without any assistance from the bodily sense-organs. (Previous experience of the deliveries of the sense organs is, however, an essential preliminary.) But in the normal, waking state these mental constructions are reduced to mere occasional fragments because of the danger that would otherwise arise. In the case above quoted, for example, Mr. Spence came near to falling over the cliff because his sensory construct was pervasive and went backwards in time, showing the cliff further out to sea than it actually was.

The importance of these cases of apparitions is that they act as a peep-hole, throwing light on the construction of the human being beyond that part which is adapted for life among physical surroundings. They show that the sense-faculties are not limited in their action to purely objective causes; nor do they come to a dead end where their practical services cease. Rather, they are in practical life abstracted and specialized from a larger field: and it is important to realise this; for it is true, not only of the sensory faculties, but of the human being altogether.

Thus apparitions, as well as all sensory abnormalities, are very instructive if examined seriously: but few people do examine them seriously. The common attitude is to smile and regard them as fairy-tales or amusing stories. For common sense they are trivial and unreal; but how completely we fail to realize that in rejecting them, common sense is behaving *pragmatically* and is not presenting a balanced picture of the truth.

It is interesting to compare the visual perception of any object in the room with the apparition of a person as seen in one of the numerous 'crisis-cases' collected by the Society for Psychical Research. In a crisis-case an apparitional figure is seen of a friend at a distance, who may be seriously ill, or dying, or undergoing an accident. The event in the physical world causes the *character* of the visual experience to be what it is in both cases; but in both cases also the cause of the visual experience itself is subjective. When we look at an object our subjective experience is minutely related to the objective facts. When we see a crisis-apparition, it is somewhat different. The correspondence of what is seen with what is actually occurring at a distance is far looser and may even represent the facts symbolically. This brings home to us that the subjective element in sense-perception is not itself rigidly caused by objects in the external world or by the processes occurring in our sense-organs. There is within us an independent creator of sense-experiences of a psychological kind; and this in the case of sight, touch, hearing, etc. has been linked during our evolution with minute exactitude to physical processes in the brain. A telepathic factor can put the psychological creator of sense-imagery into action as effectively as a physical factor in the external world. A picture of visible surroundings can be created without the intervention of any external physical factor at all. Psychologists and psychiatrists deal with the creation of sense-imagery in dreams, which is wholesale and prolific; but they concentrate their attention on the underlying, psychological causes of the subject-matter of the dream and not on the interesting and important question of how the imagery is produced. The fact that some lines of research are marked out and selected, while others are passed over and ignored is in itself significant. In fact a good deal of light could be thrown on psychology by studying the unconscious behaviour of the mind of the psychologist.

The study of apparitions thus points towards the same conclusion to which phychical research in general points. It shows that the human self transcends or overflows its apparent boundary and extends beyond it—how far we cannot tell. It shows, too, how irrational and unbalanced we become whenever we venture to cross this boundary. A book by W. F. Prince, entitled *The Enchanted Boundary*,[1] was referred to on page 232 of *The Personality of Man*. This book cites many examples of the extraordinary behaviour of people when they are faced with valid evidence of paranormal happenings. They behave as though they were enchanted and arrive at conclusions in accord with their own mental constitution but quite at variance with the facts. The lesson is plain. Our minds are narrowly adapted to a single corner of reality and if we try to leave it we are hopelessly at sea.

[1] Boston Society for Psychic Research, 1928-32.

CHAPTER V

The Physical Side

IT is natural to assume, especially to-day, that science alone can reveal the nature of the universe and can do it completely. In revealing its physical character, science has undoubtedly made much progress; but it must never be forgotten that our knowledge of the physical world reaches us through the combined media of our mind and our senses, so that the mode of transmission of that knowledge lies outside the province of physical science. We must therefore be careful not to identify the external world with its appearance to ourselves. The extent of the physical universe may not be discoverable by physics: its apparent boundaries may be determined by our own limitations.

This is where psychology and psychical research begin to reveal important things; for they throw a good deal of light on our limitations, instead of plunging at once into the objective and neglecting the subjective, as the physical sciences do. In the first place, the evidence of psychical research shows that there is more of ourselves behind the scenes than appears on the surface. It shows that to accept the entire human being as a tiny spark of vacillating consciousness, wrapped up with and dependent on the body, is to accept an illusion. But this illusion is necessary if we are to have a practical and simple outlook in daily life. Many facts support the view that the human being is greater than its normal consciousness. The ancient philosophers of India saw this; and it is not too much to say that this transcendence lies at the core of religion.

Now let us look at psychical research from a rather different angle and ask the question whether, in addition to pointing to a further extension of ourselves, it points to a further extension of the world. This is not a question to be solved by objective science. It is not a matter of the extent of space or time; it turns on the capacity of our own mental and physical powers. The evidence for extra-sensory perception, rightly interpreted, carries us at once beyond space and time. It was pointed out in chapter II that the more we look into cases of 'telepathy' and 'clairvoyance' and into the experiments made on them, the plainer it becomes that telepathy is not akin to a radio message travelling through space; nor is clairvoyance a power of perceiving physical objects with a kind of pseudo-sight. Both arise out of what psychologists call the 'unconscious'; in other words, they take place in the further extension of ourselves which lies behind the scenes. It is there that we get hold of the information and pass it up to the conscious mind. It is an *internal* process: and its *modus operandi* we do not understand. 'Mind-reading' and 'object-reading' are superficial explanations that we try to force upon the facts because such explanations appeal to us. Quantitative experiments with the guessing of cards, etc., suggest these superficial explanations in terms of thought-reading and object-reading because they show practically nothing of the process but only the result; and some investigators have been misled because they have concentrated their attention entirely upon the experimental evidence.

Telepathy, if we study the evidence for it as a whole, suggests that minds are in contact with one another beyond the range of normal consciousness. It is there that telepathy occurs. Clairvoyance suggests that matter has properties beyond the range of our senses and that these properties are in touch with the mind outside normal consciousness. The phenomenon called 'psychometry', in which a sensitive person, by holding an object in his hand, can give verifiable information about its owner, suggests the same thing. What these unsensed properties of matter can be we do not know; but telepathy, clairvoyance and psychometry all point to a further extension of the world beyond the range of the senses. That is to say, these things point to the view that matter is not as it were an island but a peninsula.

Precognition suggests this also; and it does it in a more startling manner. For however we try to explain precognition, we always end up by attempting to fasten upon it some kind of explanation that agrees with the workings of our minds. We pull it into our accustomed ways of thinking. But inevitably we fail, however loth we are to admit it.

Now the important thing about psychical research is that it throws a revealing light upon *ourselves*, showing both our own limitations and those of the world we live in. It shows also that there is a very strong impulse in us to reject any hint of these limitations and to deny them stoutly. Any problem which presents itself to the mind *must* be potentially soluble by it: that is a basic axiom of instinct. But psychical research endorses the truth that our minds are limited and specialized; also that the universe extends indefinitely beyond our mental grasp. This basic fact sinks in only very slowly, not because it is complicated or difficult, but because it goes against the grain.

The evidence for the physical phenomena [1] of psychical research, which appear to violate the laws of physics, is not as clear as one could wish. Some brief examples were given in chapters 24 and 25 in *The Personality of Man*; and we shall not here add to that evidence, for the object of this volume is not so much to put forward further evidence for the paranormal but to discuss its significance. The difficulty is that fraud has often been discovered in connection with these phenomena, and no examples of one phenomenon repeated over and over again can be obtained, as would be necessary if it were to be scientifically tested.

In estimating the evidence for the physical phenomena of mediumship, we should take tight hold of ourselves if we do not wish to be deceived; for we are between two fires. On the one hand there is the risk of being deceived by the medium, and on the other there is the risk of being deceived by an instinctive tendency of rejection within ourselves. We have, in fact, to balance on a knife-edge. We must use our critical faculty and demand good evidence, watching for every possibility of fraud; and at the same time we must restrain this critical faculty when it tends to explain reasonable evidence away. We must keep an equally sharp look-out on the phenomena and on ourselves. While keeping on our

[1] Poltergeist phenomena, telekensis, levitation, 'materialization', etc. See *The Personality of Man*, chapters 24 and 25.

guard against every pitfall, we must at the same time remember that intellectual education forces upon us the conviction that everything that really happens must fit into a pattern that is intelligible to ourselves.

The deep-seated urge in the mind acts curiously. If the evidence is strong, we may admit *verbally* that strange things do happen, while at the same time we deny them in our hearts. One often comes across this sort of thing, for example, in the case of some learned person who formally admits the evidence for telepathy, but immediately afterwards flies away from the subject and re-enters into his specialist groove. Having admitted that telepathy takes place, he does not pounce on it as an outstanding discovery; he does not proceed to consider its significance for science or for philosophy, but leaves it entirely alone. He is being urged to do this by an unconscious instinct; and it is absolutely out of the question that he is occupying an impartial standpoint.

The faculty called 'psychometry', which was described on pages 176-7 of *The Personality of Man*, also suggests that there may be properties of matter which our senses do not reveal. There is plenty of evidence that certain types of sensitives, by holding an object in the hand, can make true statements about those who have owned or previously touched it. But the evidence as a whole, and notably that collected by Dr. Eugène Osty, who was director of the *Institut Métapsychique* in Paris, does not point to the view that the information has been impressed on the matter of the object as we know it; for when once contact with the object has put the sensitive in touch with those who have previously handled it, the object itself can be destroyed without affecting the sensitive's power to continue to relate facts about these persons.

This points to the view that matter possesses properties we neither see, feel, hear, taste or smell. In practical life this possibility does not occur to us (there is a good reason why it does not); but when we ask ourselves point blank whether it is likely that our senses show us all the properties of matter, free and unbiased reason answers that it is not. For the development of our senses was carried out along wholly pragmatic lines to serve us in the exacting field of the struggle for existence. It is not likely that anything unhelpful to us in this struggle would have entered into our field of perception; on the contrary, it is probable that any perception not thoroughly utilitarian would have been blacked out by nature. We know that our eyes only respond to a short range of the spectrum set up by vibrations in the aether, while our ears respond only to a limited range of vibrations of the air. The possibility at once arises that matter may possess properties that do not create physical vibrations even beyond the infra-red or ultra-violet, or in the supersonic region of air-waves, and are not of a kind we call 'physical' at all. Mme. Morel was one of the best psychometric sensitives that Dr. Osty experimented with, though there were others who possessed the faculty in a remarkable degree. After much experience he summed up the conclusions indicated by his work as follows: (1) After the sensitive, by holding the object, has once achieved psychological connection, or *rapport*, with the contactor, the object may be destroyed without affecting the sensitive's power to give information about him. (2) The material of which the object is made does not make any difference. (3) If objects used in this way are allowed to touch one another, it does not make any difference. (4) The length of time during which the owner has possessed the object or made contact with it does not matter. (5) The lapse of time since the owner last touched the object does not matter. (6) When once the sensitive has entered into the life of the owner of the object, the *whole* of that life is accessible and not merely the portion of it during which he possessed the object.[1]

No. (1) shows that the information is not stamped on the physical properties of the object, which can be destroyed by fire or in any physical manner. Nos. (2) to (5) indicate that it is not the physical material of the object that comes into play. No. (6) suggests that the role of the object is to put the sensitive in touch with the owner or with someone who has touched it.

The information may come directly from the person concerned by extra-sensory perception (including precognition). It is of

[1] *The Personality of Man*, pp. 176-7.

course clear that the object itself plays an essential role in establishing this extra-sensory relation. But the point is that it does not appear to establish this relation by means of the properties we call ' physical ', but by means of some properties which are not apparent to the senses. Psychometry, in fact, points to the view that matter has further properties which are not of a spatial kind and are not perceptible to the human senses.

It is difficult to overcome the pressure of the innate instincts in our minds which we have been discussing; but it is well worth while making an effort to do so. Let us take an illustration to help us. Think of a solid object, perhaps a cricket-ball. At first sight nothing could be more obvious than the self-contained completeness of the cricket-ball. The bowler holds it in his hand; we can see it from every side; all there is of it is surely contained within its visible boundary. But let us press the question whether there can be properties of the cricket-ball which we do not see, and which do not respond to our touch. How could there be? we are inclined to ask. Such properties, if outside its spherical boundary, would be streaming after it as it travels down the pitch. It is self-evident that the cricket-ball, as we see it, is a complete object.

Yet, just at this point, there is a vital parting of the ways. It is here that Nature, or the adapted constitution of our minds, causes us to take something as axiomatic without knowing that we are doing so. Ordinary people do this: scientists, psychologists and even philosophers do it. Where is the boundary of the cricket-ball? Where is the boundary of our world? Do we set out to explore it in a state of mental freedom? Or are we *mentally* confined to a limited region? If you ask the astronomer, he will say that there is no boundary in the external universe beyond which we cannot explore *in principle*. The range of our senses is indeed limited; but we can supplement them by means of instruments, and there is no definite limit to the range of instrumentally assisted sense-perception. The physicist similarly sees no inherent boundary in the direction of the very small. He, too, can apparently carry exploration on indefinitely by means of new instruments and ingenious devices of inference.

The philosopher, in analysing the perceptual situation, starts with that situation as given by the senses. He clarifies and analyses it; he examines what happens when we make use of our sense-organs; but he does not step back a pace behind his starting point and examine what the instinctive level of the mind has taken for granted. The result of this is that what nature presents as the absolute starting point for all inquiry is not, in fact, the true starting point. Much more would be revealed if we were to go behind it. The world of space, time and matter is not the zero line; it is only made to *appear* to be so. By means of concurrent circumstances, of which our own constitution is foremost, the physical universe, as we see it, is made to appear to be the starting point and also the goal of all investigations—it is given the specious appearance of being isolated and including all. Telescopes, microscopes and all other means of scientific inquiry add to knowledge only within the range that has been given this false appearance of being the all-in-all.

Now the cricket-ball, like every other object, appears to be complete. We cannot imagine that it has properties that are not contained within its spherical boundary, and which trail about after it as it rushes about in space. But this is just where instinct controls our minds. The cricket-ball may have properties which do not exist in space and therefore do not trail about after it. It may have properties also which do not endure in time. Such properties would not be confined within the spherical boundary of the ball, nor would they exist in space *outside* that boundary. It requires disciplined reflection to enable us to grasp this, and in so doing to overcome the instinctive urge to deny the possible existence of such properties. But if we succeed in thinking in a balanced manner, the physical world, and indeed the universe as a whole, changes its perspective. We then see the physical world of space and time as no more than an abstracted aspect of the whole, which has been cleverly isolated by Nature. It has been given this appearance of isolation in order that finite beings with very limited minds should be able to live in it. The analyses and explorations of scientists and philosophers begin *after* the assumptions which Nature forces upon us have been made.

As we have seen above, psychometry points to the existence of properties of matter which are not detectable by physical means, and are not in themselves physical. The modern subject of psycho-somatics also points in the same direction. Even modern researches in physics suggest the same thing; for researches which attempt to discover the ultimate nature of matter lead to the discovery that the further matter is investigated the less like matter it becomes. In other words, what we call 'matter' is only a special aspect of something much greater than matter. Matter is not a complete entity, but a selection of properties from something that may possess an indefinite number of further properties, many of them quite unlike the properties that we perceive. If this is the case, the problem of psycho-physical relations is quite altered; for mind and matter may be united behind the scenes, where matter has ceased to be matter-like and perhaps has properties of a partly mental kind. The lower, instinctive phases of mind, and what we call 'life', may also have properties which are closely assimilated to the un-detected properties of matter. In fact, the whole problem of mind and matter is entirely altered if we refuse to accept the illusion that both are self-contained entities as the sense-world presents them.

The sordid phenomena of physical mediumship, despite the difficulty of securing good evidence for them, need not, on this view be regarded as a fantastic improbability. They would mean that the established laws of physics hold only in a certain region where the background-properties of matter do not interfere. But in the presence of an abnormal psycho-physical combination, these laws no longer hold. The region in which they hold has been temporarily invaded.

The assumption that the external world embraces everything flies in the face of every probability; so that the first step we have to take in order to gain true knowledge is to realize our own situation. The probability that we are right in accepting the sense-world as the one and only starting point in an attempt to discover the nature of the universe is very slight. The boundary of our world is not to be found in seeking the limits of space or time; it lies in the limitations that have been imposed upon *ourselves.* There is, in fact, no boundary to the universe. The properties of matter that we do not perceive are integral with those we do, but are rendered imperceptible and, in fact, obviously non-existent to us by the way in which our minds are constituted.

The illustration of the cricket-ball shows the subtlety of the trap which Nature has laid for us. What could have been rendered more obvious than that the cricket-ball is a complete object? How can it possess unseen properties which render it continuous with everything? It can and probably does; but it *must* appear discontinuous if the world made up of objects like it is to be sufficiently simple for limited beings to live in. Separate entities, falling naturally into separate categories and having simple space and time relations with one another, form a suitable home for simple man and a prepared school for elementary thought. If the underlying continuity of everything were obvious, the world would not present clear-cut issues and all would be too difficult to comprehend.

Matter in molar masses lends itself to the illusions of discontinuity and self-completeness, which are a necessity for the mind of simple man; and the way in which his mind and senses were evolved force this illusion upon him with tremendous power. Even when the human intellect begins to form, these basic features of adaptation condition the growing mind. That is why there is a universal tendency to dismiss as rubbish evidence for anything at variance with what the senses reveal.

When this situation is realized, we begin to see where the real boundary of our world lies. It is not in the abysses of space, nor can the theory of space-time reveal it, nor is it to be found in the ultra-microscopical world of protons and electrons. There is no boundary intrinsically existent in the universe. All is continuous *ad infinitum;* but the way we are ourselves constructed limits what we perceive and forces upon us the necessary illusion that we perceive the whole. Actually we perceive a very special and limited aspect of reality in a very special way. This should be the initial starting point of every science and of all philosophy; but it is not taken into account because it is unperceived.

Let us think over the situation. We can see what the human mind is doing. It is acting on an innate impulse to reject anything strange; for that which does not fit easily into the familiar world seems to it fantastic and bizarre. It does not adopt this attitude only towards the paranormal. Its attitude to the paranormal is merely one telling example of the way in which the mind is constructed.

CHAPTER VI

Our Mental Attitude in Science and Thought

ONCE it is realized that the human mind was impregnated with invisible factors during its evolution, which prevent it from viewing everything from an impartial standpoint, its attitude towards the unexpected becomes a matter of supreme importance. On the level of practical thought, the mind thinks in accordance with the plan of its surroundings: but it is blind to its own specialized structure. If it were suggested to a scientific specialist that the structure of his mind prevents him from seeing the whole scope of things as they are, he would probably reply that this cannot be so or science would not have made the successful progress it has done. Its outstanding achievements, he would say, afford the clearest possible proof that all that human mind discovers is true. The answer to this is that the greater part of scientific success has been achieved in the practical field, where success results from the basic fact that the mind is an instrument previously adapted by nature to work in unison with its subject-matter. In the theoretical field, progress in discovery has also been made; but there the progress has been of a different kind from that in the practical field. For one hypothesis after another has been put forward, only to be discarded later on. This was because the hypotheses were founded partly on facts 'discovered' but not wholly understood and partly on the structure of the investigator's mind. The result has been that in the field of theoretical science, investigation does not reach finality as in the practical sphere, but goes on indefinitely; and as it goes on it becomes less and less intelligible. The mind and its structure is the central factor in this.

The paranormal phenomena investigated by psychical research lie further outside the field which the mind is capable of exploring than does the subject-matter of other sciences; therefore the attitude which the human mind adopts towards the paranormal

6

is of the highest interest and importance. Examples of this attitude were given in chapters 26 and 27 in *The Personality of Man*.

When one considers how far-reaching and important the consequences of this paranormal evidence are, one immediately asks why every inquiring mind has not been filled with a desire to probe them to the limit. Evidence collected in psychical research points to a whole vista of highly significant things—knowledge conveyed without the help of the senses; the future in some inscrutable way open to human knowledge; depths of the subconscious which extend human personality indefinitely. Why does not even the barest hint of such things excite the interest of every intelligent person and fill him with an urge to explore? The evidence already collected is far more than a bare hint. For three quarters of a century evidence has been carefully collected and reinforced by experiment; yet the reaction to it is not an eager desire to carry the work further and learn all that can be learnt from it. Such interest as there is is casual and the majority tend to explain the evidence away rather than to augment it. There is not the slightest tendency to regard it as a foundation on which to build some of the most important products of human knowledge.

Extra-sensory perception illuminates in two directions. It shows that the human being transcends its everyday consciousness very widely; and it shows also that the universe extends beyond the space-time framework, which is open to the senses. It thus provides two fundamental starting points for discovering more about the universe and about ourselves. Why does not this opportunity raise tremendous enthusiasm in the mind of every pure scientist and of every philosopher and, indeed, in the mind of anyone who thinks at all? These two points are very relevant to many branches of science and to a host of philosophical problems. We cannot explain this lack of enthusiasm by saying that the evidence for the paranormal is too poor to merit serious attention; for that is certainly not the case. The *Proceedings* and *Journal* of the Society for Psychical Research, as well as the literature of certain other bodies, are full of evidence that has been collected with the utmost care. Besides, the evidence that reached the standard needed for publication there are files full of interesting cases that have never seen the light because the evidence was regarded as not being fully up to standard. The unenthusiastic behaviour of those who belittle the paranormal is not the result of the quality of the evidence; for, even if the evidence were in fact poor, the rational thing to do would be to spend effort in improving it. Reflection on this strange situation inevitably fixes the inquirer's attention on the minds of the critics. It is there that the root of the paranormal problem lies and possibly the root of other problems as well. Something is obviously influencing their minds without their knowing it. What is that 'something'? A very illuminating fact about the attitude of those who reject or ignore evidence for the paranormal is that they are perfectly logical and rational about matters in ordinary life and in the departments in which they are specialists; but they become vague and irrational when confronted with the paranormal. They do not weigh the evidence in a balanced manner, but shape their arguments so as to explain it away. Innuendo, suggestion and hints as to what may have happened take the place of an even judgement on what *did* happen. Concrete work with positive results is not accepted as conclusive evidence. Some minor flaw which does not affect the work as a whole or some derogatory incident in the life of the experimenter will be inflated and turned by innuendo into a suggestion that something is wrong with the work somewhere.

The critic who adopts this procedure with the paranormal would not dream of applying it to anything normal. If he did, he would be ridiculed and ignored; but it is regarded as rational to treat the paranormal as a kind of joke. The scientific methods employing impartial judgement and close observation are treated as being applicable only to what is called the 'normal': they are not treated as being applicable universally.

Three instances were quoted on page 241 of *The Personality of Man* in which it was said that the scientific method when used in psychical research is 'trying to prove' something. Also on page 237 Dr. Ivor L. Tuckett was quoted as saying: 'We know that the Society for Psychical Research was founded in order to establish the existence of telepathy. Therefore it is fair to consider that those early members of the Society for Psychical Research were biased in favour of telepathy.'

People do not adopt this attitude with regard to research into the normal. When astronomers look through a powerful telescope and discover a new star, no one says that they are 'trying to prove' that a new star exists. It is the structure of the human mind which behaves differently in the field of so-called rational thought *according to the assumptions with which it starts.* In a passage quoted on page 232 of *The Personality of Man*, Professor Jastrow, faced with the evidence for telepathy, piles up a grotesque conglomeration of normal factors in order to explain telepathy away. But all this is abstract and generalized; he does not attempt to show how these factors apply to actual facts. On page 238 it was pointed out that Dr. J. E. Coover and Professor L. T. Troland had carried out quantitative experiments in extra-sensory perception and reported that their results showed nothing but chance. A re-examination of their figures showed that the odds against chance reached some thousands to one. What is so interesting about this is that it was not a deliberate falsification of results, but the subconscious conviction in their minds that the paranormal could not exist caused them *unconsciously* to deflect their mathematical technique so that it would support their foregone conclusion.

These are only a few examples of the reaction which evidence for the paranormal produces on the human mind. It can be seen at once that if such a reaction exists (and the evidence for it is overwhelming) a shaft of light is thrown on a factor of paramount importance. Reason, on the intellectual level, can be deflected by innate convictions which are deeply rooted in the mind but which remain hidden beneath the surface. Immediately the question arises as to whether this is confined to the field of the paranormal or whether it operates in other fields as well. Is it not possible that this factor is universally operative, playing a part in the world's perennial troubles? Could not truly balanced reason always avoid war by making negotiations of a sensible kind? But war has gone on throughout history because balanced reason is the possession only of a few. What is it, then, which unbalances it? The intellect is not an immaculate factor of the self, seated above the arena of strife. It is down in the world of turmoil, assailed by animal instinct from below though also raised by intuition from above.

This throws a new light on the common attitude to the paranormal; *for it is not confined to the paranormal;* its basis is far wider. The human mind tends to reject *anything* that removes it from its instinctive outlook. This is worthy of deep consideration. Why, if there is a psychological urge to reject evidence for anything unfamiliar, has it not been recognized by psychologists as one of the fundamental characteristics of mind? Such an urge must be based on *instinct* which is inherited from our animal predecessors in the beginning; but later incorporated into human mentality where unobtrusively it deflects reason in predetermined directions. It is a racial characteristic, whereas psychology for the most part deals with individual tendencies and complexes and has practical rather than exploratory ends in view. At first sight it might appear that the indoctrination of reason by instinct would be obvious or would at any rate be revealed by critical analysis of the human being. But would it, if the tendency were universally installed in everyone? For the conditioning factor would be at work in the critic's mind as well as in the subject of his criticism.

One important point about instinctive reactions is that we respond to them unconsciously. The mind impelled by instinct would be convinced *by* that instinct that it was behaving in a perfectly balanced manner, while all the time it was being swayed by a subjective influence leading it to a foregone conclusion. Only by rising to the intuitive level could the deflecting instinct be detected. The mind, on the intellectual level, unaware of its hidden controls, can evolve close arguments with a high degree of cleverness, which seem to it to be perfectly balanced while they are not; but a single flash of intuition can show that all this reasoning is out of perspective.

But there is another objection to the view that the paranormal is rejected because unperceived instinct is urging us to reject it. The attitude of *nonchalance* and the tendency to ignore the findings of psychical research and to explain them away does not apply to everyone. There has always been a minority which recognized their value. This, however, does not prove that to accept or to reject the paranormal is a purely individual matter. A racial tendency to reject it is present in all; a few individuals have succeeded in rising to a level of awareness sufficiently high to enable them to overcome this racial tendency. This mastering of the universal tendency of the mind in varying degrees by individual illumination or awareness accounts for the differing attitudes of people towards the subject. But underneath these attitudes lies the universal structure of the mind, present in all.

A number of people, notably those who call themselves Spiritualists, accept the paranormal with readiness, or at least appear to do so. This fact will naturally lead to the objection that the supposed racial instinct cannot exist because it is not universal. In Spiritualists, it would be said, it is obviously lacking. But is it? It is worth while to look into this a little more closely. A basic and unconscious resistance to the paranormal has more than one way of dealing with the evidence. The first and most usual way is to turn away from it and ignore it. The second way (when the evidence becomes strong) is to pick holes in it and explain it away by specious arguments. But there is a third method. That which is unacceptable to the mind because it does not fit in with the normal can be rendered acceptable by *drawing it into the field of the normal*. This is precisely what Spiritualists do, if we may speak of them in general terms without going into their differences. If a communicator through a medium can be thought of as a person little changed from what he was in this world, using the medium as a psychic telephone, and if he is conceived of as existing in a world similar in principle to this one, then the instinct which urges mankind to accept the physical universe as the whole is not affronted any more than it would be by the discovery of a new continent.

An extraordinary compromise is effected by the mind which lies between the impact of instinct from below and intuition from above. While intuition causes the mind to be aware that reality extends beyond the sphere of the visible and makes it plain that there is a spiritual world and a genuine basis for religion, instinct draws this intuitive awareness into its own physical purview and turns the soul into a somatic conception and the continuation of reality into a physical heaven and hell. If we desire to make real progress in this world, we must do our utmost to rise above the grip of instinct and to grasp the light of intuition. Also the whole conception of the advance of knowledge as presented by science becomes altered when we rise up and realize that the scientific mind is to a high degree specialized and fitted to deal only with one special corner of reality.

CHAPTER VII

How Improbable is the Paranormal?

Is it possible to adopt a standpoint of real detachment and to decide how improbable the paranormal really is? It should be possible when once we are aware that deflecting instincts are at work within us and can be on the look-out for tendencies which rise up in us and try to explain things away.

Besides the modern and strictly scientific evidence for extra-sensory perception, there is, as has been mentioned above, the evidence of carefully conducted sittings with mediums; also of recorded automatic speech and writing; there is evidence of psychometry, in which contact with an object brings to the sensitive knowledge about its owner, or others who have touched it; there is the evidence for strange physical happenings in the presence of entranced mediums. And besides all this there is the very significant fact that throughout the history of the world there has been a belief in magic and divination; and the practice of astrology goes back four thousand years or more.

Brushing aside the subtle instinct which tells us that all these things are merely the outcome of superstition, let us ask how improbable they really are. A perfectly rational standpoint to adopt is to demand that, before one can accept evidence for any alleged fact, the strength of the evidence must be proportional to the improbability of the alleged fact. The key-question is, then: How improbable is the paranormal?

We are on firm ground so long as we are dealing with the physical world: we know its laws from generations of experience: science has examined these laws and analysed them. During the past three centuries it has confirmed them by means of countless experiments. It seems to us extremely unlikely that anything should break into or disrupt laws that keep on working so persistently and have been so clearly verified.

But does the paranormal involve the disruption of physical laws? At first sight it appears to do so. If a table can rise from the floor when no perceptible force is lifting it, if solid matter can pass through matter as is alleged to happen in séances of the physical type, if an object can convey information by touch, if the future can be known when it is impossible to infer it rationally—all these things seem flatly to disagree with the established laws of science.

Yet a crucial question arises here. Do these things, if it be granted that they occur, disrupt the established laws of our world; or do they merely indicate that these laws hold only within a limited area? Do we know how far the laws of the physical universe extend? We have to remember that the region of the real which lies open to our bodily senses is limited to that which is essential for life in the body. In that life we have to react with inanimate matter and with other forms of incarnate life. The limited character of the region that is open to our perception is concealed from the mind so that we regard what we see and perceive as the whole universe: we are prompted by an innate impulse to do so.

This is well worth thinking over. The world in which we live our daily lives is, in fact, in no way partitioned off or segregated from the universe as a whole. One thing after another indicates that it is continuous with the universe as a whole—just as continuous as is the whole surface of the globe beyond the horizon. But it would never do to allow this continuity to be visible to the practical mind; therefore when we were evolved in mind as well as in body to be thoroughly fitted to this material world we were so constructed that the continuity of extension of the world was rendered invisible. It was absolutely essential for practical efficiency that the scene of our life and action should be made to appear to us to be self-sufficient and all-inclusive and not continuous with reaches of reality which fade away beyond our mental grasp. This was achieved by adapting our bodies and our minds, and by blending them together with subtle efficiency.

If the laws of what we call the physical universe are not universal in their scope, then there is no reason whatever why laws of quite a different kind should not exist beyond them: and if that is the case, why should not these laws that we do not know interpenetrate into the fringe along with those we do know and cause occasional modifications in them?

This question, therefore, is fundamental: Why is it unlikely that strange and incomprehensible things should happen from time to time? If we try to consider this question with rational detachment, thrusting aside the enslaving control of assumptions prompted by instinct, which endeavour to persuade us that anything to which we are unaccustomed is impossible, the matter comes down to this. If any strange thing, alleged to occur in the field of the paranormal, *does* occur, is its origin within the world we know?

If we are in fact dealing, in everyday life and in science, with a world that contains everything, then it is impossible that this world could be influenced by anything from outside; for there is nothing outside it. Everything that occurs in the cosmos must have its cause in the world we know. If any strange and inexplicable events were alleged to occur, we should be justified in refusing to accept the evidence for them. We should be right in asserting that everything that could possibly happen would be of an order known to us. If we were absolutely sure of this premise, we should be quite justified in refusing to accept even the most telling evidence for the paranormal.

But if the case is different and the region of reality open to our senses (which we call the 'universe', thus asserting its all-inclusiveness) is related to further regions of reality with which we are not acquainted, we should not have the slightest justification in rejecting evidence for strange happenings originating beyond the scope of our senses and producing effects which sometimes came within that scope. However bizarre events belonging to the paranormal might seem to us, we should have no rational ground for rejecting them or even for regarding them as improbable.

The whole question of whether or not the paranormal is improbable rests on whether the world with which we are acquainted embraces everything that exists and on whether its principles, which we know, apply universally and include every principle there is. The sceptic who tries to explain away sound evidence for the paranormal is urged to do so by this innate conviction that the world he is acquainted with embraces everything; and therefore for him the improbability of the paranormal is practically infinite. He does not *state* this conviction: he *acts* upon it without being consciously aware that he holds it. The cause of his conviction is quite obviously non-rational, although he probably calls himself a 'rationalist'. It arises from an instinctive urge inserted into the human mind during its evolution. It is worth while reiterating the true nature of the human being to which all paranormal evidence points; and also its situation, until we have fully grasped them.

It was pointed out at the end of chapter II that psychical research is of great importance because it brings to light two salient facts, which are new to the modern outlook, but by no means new to ancient thought. One is that human beings extend far beyond the limits of the embodied self: the other is that the universe extends far beyond the limits of space and time. Everything points to the view that the happenings we call 'paranormal' originate beyond our everyday world and show through into it in a piece-meal and partial fashion. If we take all the evidence into account, telepathy is seen not to be the transference of an idea from one brain to another through space; clairvoyance not to be an extra-sensory perception of the spatial characteristics of matter; precognition not to be a leap forward along the dimension of time; mediumistic communications to be no more than a forcing of terrestrialized information through the bottle-neck of the incarnate mind. If we admit the laws of physics and the properties of matter as revealed by science and the senses to be *partial*, then the things that happen at sittings with physical mediums could well be no more than an intrusion of other laws and further characteristics outside the scope of our world but manifesting themselves occasionally within it. Indeed, what we call 'matter' may well be, not a self-complete and self-contained entity, but no more than a selection of practically useful characteristics of something that is far more pervasive; and perhaps ultimately at one with the infinite. Briefly, the evidence suggests that what is

called the 'paranormal' consists of no more than sporadic in-
filtration of laws and properties which originate outside the world
we know.

This brings us always back to the same question: Does the
universe of space and time that our senses reveal include everything? Does it extend beyond these limits, perhaps neither in
space nor in time? A subtly hidden impulse in ourselves which
works upon us like a hypnotic suggestion, tries to persuade us that
such an idea is nonsense and that there *can* be nothing beyond the
space-time universe. Obviously, it whispers to us, space and time
are the framework within which lies the whole of reality; what
more *can* there be? And we meekly yield to this impulse. We do
so by our *actions;* we make the spatio-temporal world our
starting-point; that is to say, we take it for granted as the axiomatic beginning for every inquiry without asking any questions
about it. Instinct jockeys us into it before we begin to act or to
think at all: science and philosophy begin their inquiries *after*
accepting these instinctive takings-for-granted. When we do this
we unconsciously yield to a suggestion so deeply ingrained in the
mind that it always succeeds in evading conscious criticism.
Consequently we start to investigate the world always a step too
late.

The illustration of the cricket-ball in chapter V shows how
'obvious' is the self-completeness of matter as perceived by the
senses—the extraordinarily subtle device by means of which our
world is made to appear all-inclusive: and this is forced upon us
as axiomatic. The entire doctrine of Materialism arises from this
instinctive acceptance instilled into us by nature in order to render
us practically efficient in action. It is indeed useful in practice; but
it is a complete illusion. Its subtlety gives it the false appearance of
being based on reason while in reality it is based on a self-concealed
impulse.

The study of psychical research, for those who can undertake
it without bias, can lead to a discovery of the greatest importance,
for it can act as the key to the situation in which we human beings
are placed. The ordinary man has no idea that his intellectual range
of thought, together with the range of his senses, are confined to

a tiny fragment of the universe; and that even within this fragment they are specialized through and through so that they present the fragment in a special way. That reality, untouched and unknown, surrounds him on every side, is a fact which his mind can only very slowly come to realize.

The key-question about the evidence for paranormal happenings is, then, this. How improbable are they? There is a clear and definite answer to this question; but few people are capable of attaining it, for few can view the world from an impartial standpoint. The answer which the vast majority of people accept arises from the non-rational factors with which their minds are filled.

CHAPTER VIII

The Occult

THE age-old belief in magic and the occult arouses light-hearted scepticism and often derisive criticism. An almost irresistible impulse urges us to put down the whole of the occult to superstition. But if we are able to deal with the voice within us that urges this in a critical manner, we can ask how improbable on strictly rational grounds the alleged facts of magical phenomena and the occult really are. Are they, in fact, improbable? Curiously enough modern investigations called 'psycho-somatic' are beginning to invade this ancient territory. Both the old magician and the modern psychosomatistician take seriously the view that a drop of blood, if treated in a certain way, can yield information about its owner. The modern mind reacts against anything of this kind, objecting that it is impossible; for a drop of blood, as we conceive it to-day, consists solely of a complex group of molecules existing in space. This is where we come to the point. The modern mind assumes that blood possesses only properties detectable by the human senses assisted by scientific methods—that is to say, blood exists wholly in the spatio-temporal world. But how do we know that a drop of blood has no properties lying beyond the reach of our senses? Reflection shows that we do not; but we assume it because something innate within us urges us to reject everything that our senses do not reveal. When we laugh at the idea of magic and dismiss it as superstition, it is not rational thought that urges us to do so but something innately fixed in our adapted nature. We claim that the objective knowledge gained by science shows us the whole truth; but that is a pure assumption. There is not the slightest reason why matter should not have all kinds of properties which our senses do not reveal; in fact, probability is in favour of its having them. Our senses are obviously not universal in their scope. Neither are our minds because they too have been indoctrinated so as to make the world appear much

simpler than it is. Therefore there is likely to be a great deal that
we do not perceive.

If we look at the matter from a *rational* and not from an
instinctive point of view, there is nothing improbable about
magic or the occult or the paranormal. Take astrology as an
example. This has been studied for at least four thousand years
by persons who to-day are looked upon as pre-scientific ignor-
amuses. Our assumption is that throughout this vast period
they merely exercised their imagination and never obtained any
results that would justify them in continuing the study. What
moon-struck idiots they must have been! Is astrology improbable
fron the rational standpoint? The answer 'Yes' is based on the
assumption that the principle of causality which runs through the
physical world we know extends throughout the entire universe.
According to astrology, the positions of heavenly bodies as seen
from the earth are correlated with the lives and characteristics
of human beings. Nothing could seem more absurd when seen
from the causal standpoint. But suppose that, besides or beyond the
causal principle there is a pattern running through things in which
sequences of events are related to one another without being
causally connected. This strikes us as absurd. Why should one
chain of events be correlated with another unless there is something
to account for it? The simple answer is that there may be all
kinds of things in the universe that we do not understand; probability is strongly in favour of this, but our minds are so constituted
that we reject it because we are basically urged to accept what we
perceive *as the whole*. This assumption is purely subjective; but
that is the last thing we realize.

Thus, it is probable that magic, astrology and the occult in
general are signs of an existing pattern in the universe beyond
the range of sense-perception and beyond the compass of the mind
which is adapted to it. This pattern can show through into the
world we know. It is at this very point at which the subjective
factor in us pulls down the shutter that the extension of the universe begins. It does not follow, however, that the entire universe
beyond the scope of our senses has the character of what we call
the 'occult'. That may be only one section of it. Many other things,

far higher in their nature and even more incomprehensible to our present minds, can exist beyond these marginal phenomena. In fact, the point to grasp is that the whole universe, inconceivably vast and, in fact, infinite is continuous with the portion we know. Once we endeavour to leave that portion, we leave the area to which we are adapted behind and at once we are out of our depth and we behave as if we had entered on enchanted ground.

As long ago as 1896, William James, in his presidential address to the Society for Psychical Research, made with great insight the following comments: 'Science, taken in its essence, should stand only for a method, and not for any special beliefs, yet, as habitually taken by its votaries, Science has come to be identified with a certain fixed general belief, the belief that the deeper order of Nature is mechanical exclusively, and that non-mechanical categories are irrational ways of conceiving and explaining even such things as human life.'

Owing to the advance in Physics since 1896, mechanical explanations have become somewhat outmoded; but if we substitute 'mathematical' for 'mechanical', the above statement is still substantially true.

With regard to our modern mental perspective, William James says: 'But our own *Proceedings* and *Journals* have, it seems to me, conclusively proved one thing to the candid reader, and that is that the verdict of pure insanity, of gratuitous preference for error, of superstition without an excuse, which the scientists of our day are led by their intellectual training to pronounce upon the entire thought of the past, is a most shallow verdict. . . . When from our present advanced standpoint we look back upon the past stages of human thought, we are amazed that a Universe which appears to be of so vast and mysterious a complication should ever have seemed to anyone so little and a plain thing. Whether it be Descartes' world or Newton's; whether it be that of the Materialists of the last century or that of the Bridgewater treatises of our own; it always looks the same to us—incredibly perspectiveless and short.'

William James was a man of insight. He saw through the conviction which science had spread so widely in his day and which still persists in our own—the conviction that it is providing us with an outline picture of the entire universe. What lies within the range of our restricted senses, and still more what lies within the range of our specialized intellect, is indeed 'perspectiveless and short'! While science is genuinely unfolding one particular corner of the universe, it has succumbed to the great illusion that it is unfolding the whole. At the bottom of this illusion lies the adapted nature of the human being and the fact that its adaptation is hidden from its own consciousness.

A very telling illustration of this was once brought out in a short story by H. G. Wells, entitled *The Country of the Blind*. This story reflects human nature as in a mirror, showing how it reacts to evidence that proves the universe to extend far beyond the known world and that proves also the existence of things that differ widely from those to which we are accustomed.

This story tells how in the wilds of the Andes in Ecuador a fertile valley had for generations been cut off from the rest of the world by a gigantic landslide, which blocked the only means of approach from the outer world. The inhabitants of this valley managed to support themselves by what they grew; but as time went on a disease developed among them, which produced gradual blindness. As their sight faded generation by generation, their sense of hearing, touch and scent became intensely acute, so that they still succeeded in carrying on the tasks of daily life. They constructed paved paths across their fields, which were numbered by notches; and by means of these they found their way without difficulty to any point in their territory.

One day a mountaineer named Nuñez from the country near Quito acted as a guide to a party of Englishmen who were climbing the Andes. Suddenly Nuñez disappeared. He had slipped and fallen down the vast slopes on the eastern side of the mountains and was precipitated down hundreds of feet of steep snow-slopes until finally he found himself in the fertile valley of the blind. Bewildered at first, he after a time gained confidence and began to explore the valley. He found huts were windowless and built with patchy walls of odd colours; and then, meeting some of the inhabitants, he realized that they were blind. In order to keep up

7

his courage in this strange environment, he kept on repeating to himself: In the country of the blind the one-eyed man is king! But as time went on he found that this was not the case.

The blind inhabitants were not unfriendly, but the enormous advantage of his sight was not recognized by them. In fact, they treated him as an oddity. He explained to them as best he could that he possessed the sense of sight; but they replied that this word did not mean anything, and they asked him where he had come from. Obviously to them he came from the fringe of the world, somewhere beyond the rocks which bounded it: for the blind believed that their valley embraced the whole realm of existence. There was nothing beyond it: how could there be?

Nuñez tried to convince them that he could see all kinds of things around him, and in his explanation he argued desperately: but in his excitement he stumbled over a bucket that one of them had put down and this convinced them of the poor quality of his senses; for they themselves controlled their movements with the greatest precision. 'He is but newly formed', said one of them. 'He stumbles as he walks and mingles words that mean nothing with his speech.'

They took him to a conference in one of their houses to consider what his future status should be among them. The room was windowless and dark and Nuñez stumbled over his companions. This confirmed the blind men in their opinion that he was abnormal and elementary. In no way could Nuñez convey to them the nature of sight or convince them of its existence. Their whole conception of things was a product of their own sensory capacities, and nothing that he said to them did anything to change or enlarge it. 'Blind men of genius had arisen among them and had questioned the shreds of belief and tradition they had brought with them from their seeing days and had dismissed them all as idle fancies.' Nuñez tried to convince them that they were not idle fancies but real. 'He spoke of the beauties of sight, of watching the mountains, of the sky and the sunrise, and they heard him with amused incredulity; but presently became condemnatory. They told him there were indeed no mountains at all but that the end of the rock where the llamas grazed was indeed the end of the world;

thence sprang a cavernous roof over the universe, from which the dew and the avalanches fell; and when he maintained stoutly that the world had neither end nor roof such as they supposed, they said his thoughts were wicked.'

At last one of the ablest members of the blind community thought of a way in which the abnormalities of Nuñez might be cured. There is something affecting his brain, he said. When the others asked what it was he replied that it was undoubtedly the queer things called eyes—those soft depressions in the face. In the case of Nuñez, he said, they are diseased: they are distended and the eyelids move and this causes constant irritation to the brain. But a simple surgical operation could remove these irritant bodies and Nuñez would then become sane.

The wise man was universally applauded. 'Thank heaven for science', said one of the company. They told Nuñez of the good fortune that was coming to him by means of the relieving operation. Steeped in gloom, he went out to take a last look at the beauties of nature with which he was surrounded. There was the sunshine, the blue sky and the glory of the everlasting snow. Suddenly he made up his mind and, turning his face to the mountains, he began to climb.

What an allegory this story is! It reflects the. human race as in a mirror. Our whole conception of the universe is determined as strictly as that of the blind people by our own characteristics, perceptions and limitations. Any evidence of more beyond those limits is rejected and explained away just as the blind people explained away evidence of an extended world beyond the rocky boundary of their valley. Anyone with a high faculty of intuition or mystical insight is dismissed as morbid just as Nuñez was on account of his sight. Nuñez's descriptions of the mountains that they could not see were treated as a fairy-tale because there was an innate conviction that forced upon them the conclusion that what they could experience was all. They thought of the sky as a smooth surface of rock because the end of all things must be something potentially accessible to the sense of touch. We do exactly the same when we look for the confines of the universe in that which appeals to the sense of sight—the depths of space explored by astronomy. It is important to note that it was not lack of evidence that made them refuse to believe that Nuñez could see. The evidence was there, but they twisted it till they made it conform to their preconceived notions. That is just what we do. It is pure illusion to imagine that we can extend a balanced and poised mind to anything beyond the range of our senses. We force facts obtained by scientific methods to fit in with our common-sense outlook despite its obvious limitations, and only very gradually, as facts accumulate, does the scientific outlook become enlarged and force itself a little further away from that of common sense. Only with extreme slowness does it dawn upon us that our ordinary outlook is narrow, specialized and founded on our own mental and physical constitution. The current view about the nature of mind is a case in point. The brain is assumed to embrace the causes of the mind because the brain is accessible to our senses and therefore a field for ex-periment. Mind must be a function of brain, or at least in some way brain-dependent in its origin. If not, it would be isolable by experiment and detectable as a separate entity. This is the type of reasoning pressed upon us by the adapted nature of our minds which urges us to accept as obvious that the world of the senses contains the causes of everything and that anything which exists at all must be accessible and intelligible to us. It is the same kind of reasoning that the blind folk used to discredit the assertions of Nuñez. They could not believe that there were things in principle perceptible far beyond the range of their limited senses of hearing and touch. If such things were there at all, they *must* be capable of being heard or felt. Telepathy and extra-sensory perception show that the mind can work in independence of the brain; but this evidence is brushed aside because it does not fit in with the general sense-picture necessary for practical life.

All this shows how much that we believe to be impartially rational we accept on unconscious impulse and afterwards use as the premises of reason. It throws a vivid light on the fundamental irrationality which underlies the doctrine called 'Rationalism'. Once we have realized that many things *do* pass beyond our powers of comprehension, it is vitally important that we should free our minds sufficiently to see clearly where this happens. If the apparent all-inclusiveness and self-completeness of the sensible world is realized to be an unconscious assumption of our own, the whole universe begins to fall into true perspective. This realization is the essential starting point from which to begin any exploration of reality which is to lead to truth. The flat, perspectiveless picture which is produced by science then becomes three-dimensional; and only in this way can we truly understand what science is, what it is doing, what are its limitations and how much subjectivity it unconsciously includes. In fact, when it has been realized that our mental adaptation to our world is a fact and some glimpse of the vast consequences of this adaptation has been achieved, our entire conception of man and the universe is changed. At present, our world is like the lighted stage of a theatre, which rivets all attention upon itself and dismisses all thoughts of what lies beyond.

A very instructive thing to note is that the blind men could not believe that the world extended beyond the rocky confines of their valley. The distant mountains and cities of which Nuñez tried to convince them were dismissed as rubbish; and we do exactly the same kind of thing. If we look into it impartially we can see the reason for it; for success and whole-hearted confidence in everyday life depends on complete absorption in the world in which we have to act; there must be nothing to distract us from it or to give rise to disturbing *arrière pénsées*. This could only be achieved by making it appear obvious that this visible world includes everything. All must be clear-cut and self-complete. But merely to have this idea is not enough: it has to be forcibly embedded in the mind by the power of *instinct*, acting in a way similar to hypnotic suggestion. This mental fixation not only operates in practical life; it rises upwards and permeates the intellect, deeply influencing science and philosophy.

Certain objections to the view that the tendency to reject the paranormal arises from primitive instinct are likely to be raised. One of these is that primitive man was presumably to a very large extent swayed by instinct; yet he accepted the paranormal more readily than we do. If instinct was urging him to accept the physical world about him as the all-in-all, how did his ready acceptance of the spirit world come about? But primitive man, as we know him from the records, *was* really man and had risen far above the animals. As man he therefore possessed the spectrum-like mind which we possess: that is to say, his mind, like ours, lay at the meeting point of instinct acting from below and intuition acting from above. He was under the influence of both; and perhaps in a way he was more open to intuition than we are: for intellectualized society has the effect of damping intuition down. We should probably have to go back half a million years or so to find man so near the animal world that he could not be influenced by intuition.

CHAPTER IX

Normal and Paranormal are One

THE most fundamental fact to grasp about things called 'paranormal' is that they are not a segregated class of phenomena—they are not isolated or existing alone, but arise from faculties which are universally present in mankind. It is true that they emerge in different degrees in different individuals; but, under the surface, they are part of the universal structure of all human beings. We regard them askance because they reveal things which do not wholly fit into this world; and we do not grasp the central fact that this world is no more than a tiny speck in the whole of reality. The apparent queerness of the things that filter through from beyond the confines of the ordinary world is not *intrinsic* queerness; it is solely relative, and seems queer to us only from our special point of view. Anything quite different from the things we are accustomed to is bound to seem queer and incredible to us. It is strictly irrational to reject evidence for anything because it seems queer; for the most unlikely thing from a truly rational standpoint is that the things we are accustomed to include the whole of the universe. Paranormal faculties and paranormal phenomena cannot be ignored if we wish to form a true notion of what man really is; for these are key-phenomena from the point of view of giving useful information. The study of the paranormal should be regarded as an attempt to gain a truly balanced picture of the human being and not as a ridiculous study of queer oddities, existing (if at all) apart from the things that matter in a little province of their own. By ignoring the paranormal we are in fact building a *selective* and not a truly comprehensive picture of ourselves.

The object of the present little book is to estimate the significance of the paranormal, of which examples were given in *The Personality of Man*. The attempt to do this has inevitably carried us into a larger field and involved our entire outlook on the universe. It is because the human mind is specially adapted to its world that it concentrates its attention like a search-light on that world and refuses to recognize it as being a parochial fringe of reality. Paranormal faculties and paranormal phenomena are just as 'normal' from the larger point of view as are the everyday faculties and phenomena we call normal; but these faculties belong to outlying regions of the self as it appears in this world and they act into this world more or less sporadically. The existence of the paranormal points to a further reach of selfhood beyond the self of daily life and to an extension of the universe beyond the reach of science.

The great value of psychical research is that it has begun to put perspective into the universe and to show us that neither we nor our world come to an end where we thought they did.

It is not only the paranormal, however, which shows this. The higher faculties of intuition and inspiration show it too: so does the self that has achieved elevation to the heights of mysticism. The universal tendency in man in all ages and all places to turn to religion shows it also, however grotesquely the impulse may sometimes be crystallized when drawn down to the level of the adapted mind. Psychical research has shown with the utmost clearness that extra-sensory perception exists; but it shows a further thing of great importance, namely that its source lies deep in the self beyond the normal self and is beyond our reach and probably beyond our comprehension. It shows also that very striking communications sometimes arrive through mediums; but they are enigmatic when looked into and they invite many questions. They are divided into different grades. Psychical research shows also that material objects have some properties which enable a sensitive to make true statements about facts concerning them and their owners; but these properties of matter also lie outside the field of experimental science. This shows that something beyond ordinary physical laws must belong to matter. All these things undoubtedly occur; but they do not flatly contradict general experience or what science has discovered. They indicate only that general experience and scientific research are working within the confines of a limited field; and things which occur outside this field in certain circumstances intrude into it.

What is of great importance is that we start with an ingrained conviction which causes us in the present day to do the same sort of things that medieval thinkers did when they formed a picture of the physical universe. They took it for granted that the earth was the centre of the universe and that the sun, moon and stars revolved around it as its attendants. We similarly take it for granted that our normal consciousness is the centre and the whole of us, and that the physical cosmos revealed by the senses and further explored by science constitutes the entire universe. In other words, what we are familiar with *must* be central. This natural assumption is forced upon us by our combined mental and physical constitution; and behind it lie all the adaptive forces of evolution. But science has strongly reinforced this instinctive assumption by accepting it as the basis on which to build. When this simplifying and (from the point of view of knowledge) illusory instinct begins to give way to the higher grades of awareness and insight, the true situation begins to dawn. Perspective, abolished from the world by Nature for practical reasons, makes its first appearance and our conception of the cosmos begins to fall into shape. This change of outlook is of a Copernican order, though on a vastly larger scale; for it does not deal with the spatial universe alone.

The two following small cases from psychical research illustrate the lack of any real distinction between normal and paranormal. The first is the case of a man who habitually went to a club-room in the evening and, in order to get there, had to pass through a field-gate. Time after time he saw the bars of the gate several feet before he came to it. His sense of sight was hallucinated. The second was the case of a person who was in bed and, on waking, saw the name of a relation written on the pillow. Soon afterwards news arrived of this relation's death; but the person who saw the name had had no reason to expect it. Both accounts rest on equally good first-hand evidence and both are examples of what is called hallucination of the senses.

In spite of their similarity, our minds urge us to assign these two cases to quite different categories. The first we would call 'normal' and we would accept it at once, even on slight evidence. The second we would call 'paranormal' and we would demand evidence of a much more stringent kind before accepting it. Many would, no doubt, try to explain the second case away while accepting the first case as a matter of course. This assignment of the two cases to different categories is due to a *subjective* cause in ourselves—in this case to the degree of improbability we subjectively assign to telepathy.

This behaviour of the human mind is not confined to the field of psychical research, although in that field it is strikingly illustrated. The mind always reacts to an impulse which penetrates it through and through, forcing upon it the conviction that the sense-world is complete in itself. If we can rise above this innate conviction and see things more impartially, it becomes evident that there is no dividing boundary between the normal and the paranormal; and there is no reason (apart fron our instinctive urge) to regard the paranormal as less probable than the normal. The apparent boundary consists in the limited boundary of our senses, reinforced by the instinct which convinces us that that boundary is objective and not subjective. In point of fact, the division between normal and paranormal, or between the ordinary and the occult, or between the natural and the supernatural—whatever terms we choose to use—does not exist. It is our own mental constitution which creates for us the illusion that they are there. The universe is through and through a continuity; but our constitution fixes our attention upon one small fragment of it, and presents this fragment as the whole. There is no real boundary between the two—no reason why we should try to explain the 'supernatural' away: no reason why we should assign the source of religion to primitive imaginings. It is to *ourselves* that we should turn our attention; we should study the evolutionary formation of our minds if we wish to form a true outlook on the universe.

Edwyn Bevan takes a wide survey of the paranormal or supernatural realm in his book, *Sybils and Seers*. He describes it, for the most part, as it appeared in classical times. Referring to the

experiences of the Indian Christian, Sadhu Sundar as 'imagery
made up of traditional material', he goes on to say: 'What it
comes to is this: even if in such an experience there is an appre-
hension of some reality beyond the mind of the visionary, his
recollection of it, the account of it he gives to others, is fused
with a mass of ideas and images which were in his mind—whether
by tradition or in some other way—quite apart from the vision.
An Orphic who had such an experience might tell afterwards of
Charon, and the springs on either side of the road, and the tall
cypress-tree, and so on; but that would be all imagery which he
brought to the experience, not knowledge he had got from the
experience. When you abstract all these ideas and images—the
form as Canon Streeter calls it—what is left? I throw out as a
suggestion that nothing is left which can properly be called
knowledge, and yet that the experience has a value. It seems to be a
characteristic of the mystical ecstasy—of which, I take it, these
apparent visits to the spirit-world are one variety—that it gives an
immense sense of knowing, of marvellous clarity, without any
definite thing known. You will find it described in the last canto
of the *Paradiso:* it appeared in recollection to Dante that in the
supreme moment the whole universe had lain before him, an
open book, but he believes that this was so—not because he can
state some definite truth about the universe he did not otherwise
know, but because, as he speaks of that moment, he has a feeling
of expansive joy:

> La forma universal di questo nodo
> credo ch'io vidi, perche piu di largo,
> dicendo questo, mi sento ch'io godo.

If this is so, the experience may have an immense value for the
person who has gone through it; it may give to his religious
beliefs a vividness and power which nothing can afterwards
shake: he knows he laid hold of reality. But it has a value for him,
not for anyone else. It gives him no knowledge which he can
formulate and communicate. So far as he purports to give to
others, on the basis of such experience, information about the
world, that is illusion' (pp. 64-5).

The point is that paranormal experiences are not isolated into one separate category, while religious experiences are isolated in another; and at the same time the experiences of daily life are cut off and separate from both. The separation is due to our own way of looking at things. All human experiences are, in fact, graded and interwoven; but those of everyday life have been made to appear separate from everything else by a device of Nature, the object of which is to make the external world appear clear and to concentrate undivided attention upon everyday affairs.

Psychical research thus shows that the subjective element plays a much larger part in our world that we realize. It is not that there is no objective world but that the latter is subtly interwoven with subjective factors. We ourselves are a determining factor in almost all we perceive. *Our* way of thinking, *our* specialized senses, *our* mental and bodily constitution—all these lie at the root of our knowledge and general outlook. The dominating factor in it all is subjective. The objective world is a skeleton clothed and given all that is important in its character by the subjective.

Psychical research brings this subjectivity to light in a startling manner. One would expect, therefore, that no one would resist evidence for faculties which extend beyond the scope of this world without giving them careful and serious study; but the general attitude is exactly the opposite. People explain away such faculties and phenomena in the most light-hearted fashion, using arguments to dispose of them which would be merely laughed at if they applied to anything normal. Chance, for example, is widely held to be capable of explaining far more in the paranormal field than it could possibly explain in any other. This is quite irrational; but few question it. Again it is often said that no valid evidence for the paranormal exists, when all the time it does; but those who say this have not troubled to look for it. All this is clearly due to an inborn tendency in the mind to get rid of anything which does not square with what is familiar; and it is highly significant that this tendency does not adhere to rational rules. Any trumped up, illogical argument will serve to get rid of the paranormal because there is an instinctive urge behind it. This urge is universal (though individual factors vary it in degree); otherwise these arguments would be torn to pieces by criticism. Psychical research thus discloses a tendency in our selves, which, once recognized, is seen to be a matter of universal importance.

Viscount Haldane in his book, *The Pathway to Reality*, emphasized this subjectivity of which we are unaware in the following sentence: 'The claim sometimes advanced on behalf of natural science that it deals with absolute reality, independent of man himself, cannot be maintained' (p. 118). His brother, the physiologist and philosopher J. S. Haldane also referred to the 'superstitions of common sense—superstitions which arise when you try to apply what you have got in this fashion to speculative problems, which lie outside the scope of everyday reflection' (*Mechanism, Life and Personality*, p. 115). The factor behind this attitude is common sense; and common sense was brought into existence to promote an artificial clarity necessary for success in practical life. The *boundary* of this world, beyond which reality extends indefinitely, has been hidden from us by this subtle device of bringing the finite features of the world into prominence and concealing those which do not present the appearance of finality. The last thing that ever enters our minds is that the whole situation in which we live has been *arranged* in the course of our evolution.

It may take a long time for this lesson revealed by psychical research to sink in, especially in an age when stress and turmoil do not encourage quiet reflection. But the lesson is that the aim of the human intellect should be, not to discover and understand all things without limit, but to see the point at which reality passes beyond the grasp of the intellect.

What we have been considering in this book has had the effect of showing us that our real situation is quite different from that which common sense presents. Perhaps a little illustration will help still further to bring this home to us. We have to-day the wireless, the cinema and television; and progress with them all is going on apace. The cinema presents scenes in colour and attempts are already being made to produce the pictures in three dimensions so that they stand out like real places. Suppose that inventions of this kind had gone much further, so that by stepping into a suit something like a diving dress we could seem to be standing in a distant scene, its visible features conveyed by television and the sounds in it by radio, sensations of touch and smell being artificially produced by complicated devices installed in the diving dress. When we put out our hand we should apparently touch what we could see, and we should feel the ground under our feet. We should, in fact, seem to ourselves to *be* transported to a distant scene; and if one more operation were performed on us by something akin to a hypnotic suggestion and our memory of all that happened before we got into the suit were erased, we should not have the slightest doubt that we *were* actually in the scene presented to us. We should in fact be living our life in another world and should be completely unaware that our body was where it actually stood. Suppose some very alarming adventure occurred in the televised scene—an earthquake or a forest fire overtaking us —causing us to make such frantic endeavours to escape that we tore the diving suit and forced our way out of it. What an overwhelming surprise we should have! We should have apparently been flashed into another world; and then, if our memory began to return, we should realize that we had been there all the time. There is probably some faint analogy between this imaginary happening and our situation in this present world; for the whole make-up of our body and its organs of sense, combined with the adapted character of our mind, concentrate our entire attention upon the field which our senses present, much as the diving suit and its paraphernalia would translate us, to all appearances, into another world. The non-physical reality, which in fact exists all around us, is hidden in much the same way as the actual place in which we were standing in our diving dress would be hidden by the devices of television and radio, etc. At the end of our life in this world, it is very unlikely that we shall be shot off into another, the location of which we cannot imagine. *We are there already:* for a change of worlds is not brought about by spatial travel but by a change in what we are aware of. Our bodily construction and mental indoctrination hide this fact from us with superb efficiency.

The part played by the mind in adapting us for life in our world, and in making that world appear to include everything, is far greater than we realize. Professor J. Z. Young, in the fourth of his Reith Lectures, entitled *Doubt and Certainty in Science*,[1] broadcast in November, 1950, gave a striking example of this when he described the experiences of persons born blind who later received their sight. He spoke as though the mental factor in seeing were purely a brain-process; but that we must expect from a scientific specialist, for the mind adapted to the physical world urges us to believe that matter is the causal centre of everything; and science has taken over this assumption without criticism.

Professor Young said that the blind patient who opens his eyes to the world for the first time gets little or no enjoyment from his experience. 'Indeed he finds it painful.' No separate objects stand out in the visual field among the mass of coloured patches, which is all that is at first revealed. If asked what is the shape of an orange, the patient says: 'Let me touch it and I will tell you!' 'The real point is that what these people lack is the store of rules in the brain, rules usually learnt by the long years of exploration with the eyes during childhood.' But 'rules in the brain' stand for the mind's contribution to seeing. Until the mind sees a group of coloured patches as an object, to see the external world is impossible. It is true that the mind's action is normally closely associated with brain-processes. But brain-processes are not the whole cause of our perceptions; for the activities of matter situated in space, however complex, are not identical with subjective experience. Of course we cannot regard the brain as one entity and the mind as another, equally isolable and equally comprehensible. Mind is not identical with brain: but neither can it be trapped and pigeon-holed and made to become a quarry of scientific exploration. It is an entity belonging to a totally different category.

The subjective factor in sense-perception is thus amazingly important. 'Many of our affairs are conducted on the assumption

[1] Oxford University Press.

that our sense-organs provide us with an accurate record, independent of ourselves. What we are now beginning to realize is that much of this is an illusion; that we have to learn to see the world as we do.'

Again, Professor Young's view endorses what was said in chapter IV, pages 56, 60, about the immensely prolific possibilities of sensory hallucinations and their power of creating complete surroundings when the mind is not in a state of waking alertness. Environments which are completely realistic can be created by subconscious levels of the mind. To quote Professor Young's words: 'These ways of acting that we learn give us a rhythm of behaviour. Remember the brain is not a passive mass of tissue. Through all waking life it drives along. Woken in the morning by some stimulus, it immediately begins to run through sequences of activities, according to the rules it has learned. These sequences produce the actions by which the body lives. They are partly touched off by outside stimuli, but once started, they may run by themselves as independent trains in the brain, each combination starting another one.'

This example of the effect of the acquisition of sight by an adult brings home to us the extraordinary thoroughness of our adaptation to our surroundings. It knocks out the conviction which nature has implanted in our minds that we perceive the universe quite simply and directly without intermediary processes. It reveals the fact that we only perceive a small corner of it and that in a highly specialized manner. But the important point to remember is that we are not *wholly* adapted in this way; our minds do not lie *wholly* within the adapted area: they transcend the area of adaptation, level above level, by gradation, and in this way they leave adaptation gradually behind. To rise up as far as we can in these gradations is essential for freedom of thought and true understanding. All the upward steps in progress that the human intellect has made in the past have been the result of upward climbing towards higher awareness by the individual. What we should do is to turn to those individuals who have climbed highest and try to copy them.

The whole of psychical research as well as the psychiatric branch of psychology point to a conclusion which is of enormous importance. They show that the human mind or self is not confined to that portion of it which operates in daily life, but extends far beyond its apparent limits. The boundary of the normal self is not an edge where the self comes to an end, but is the limit of an abstracted portion of the self that has been withdrawn from the whole and concentrated on the physical world.

We usually think of ourselves as compact, little entities, neatly rounded off and entirely separated from others. The mind or self or being (whatever we choose to call it) is assumed to be as monadic in character as the body. But that is an illusion fostered by nature for the sake of clarity. We see, hear and feel from the isolated standpoint of the body; and our actual integration with others and with the universe at large is concealed from us as if by a shutter.

Precognition appears quite naturally in all kinds of experience which originate outside the normal sphere of consciousness; and this suggests something further than an extension of ourselves. It suggests that the world we live in is as far from including the whole universe as our practical consciousness is from including the whole of ourselves. For precognition cannot originate in the world we know; nor can it be the consequence of brain-processes. In this world it is a misfit, incompatible with its principles, especially with that of temporal causality. Thus, when we pass beyond the range of our senses, we find evidence that both we and the world we live in have been given a specious appearance of self-completeness. This does not merely mean that the human senses are limited; it means that the practical mind has been formed in such a way that it reinforces the impression given by the senses and takes for granted things which are not true, but which make for simplicity and efficiency in practical life. This is not an exceptional tendency which shows itself in an individual here and there, but a general human tendency, although its power varies in different individuals according to their degrees of insight. It is important to notice that it is *subjective* and therefore undermines the principle of what is supposed to be objective

8

research, but it is part of its nature that this should be hidden from view.

An interesting book by W. F. Prince, called *The Enchanted Boundary*, was referred to in *The Personality of Man* on page 232, and in this book it was held that evidence for the paranormal lies on the far side of the boundary, after crossing which the human mind behaves as though it were enchanted. I came to see that this boundary has no real, objective existence; it is a boundary created by our own mentality. In other words, it is only within the range of what we call the 'normal' that the human mind works in consonance with the world around it. Outside the province of the 'normal' the mind is at sea. Rejecting the canons of evidence, it arrives at conclusions that are in accordance with its own nature and not with the facts with which it is confronted. If sound and solid evidence points to the occurrence of phenomena that are utterly strange, the mind at once tries to pull them into line with the familiar and to force upon them the kind of explanations with which it is fitted to deal.

This powerful tendency in the mind which causes it to criticize the paranormal so rigorously that it explains it away, or, if the evidence is overwhelmingly strong to draw it into the ordinary world and normalize it, reminds one of party-political arguments: whatever the evidence may be, it has to be brought into line with the party outlook. The conclusion with which all evidence must conform is that the world our senses reveal contains everything there is. It was this tendency to reach foregone conclusions on the part of critics of the paranormal which brought home to me the feature of the mind which works behind the scenes. *Invisibility is part of the instinct which directs our reason.* Why have not psychologists and psychiatrists realized that this universal instinct exists and concentrates all attention on the sense-world, while it blacks out the remainder or makes it seem unreal? The answer is simple. It is because of its universality; it is because psychologists and psychiatrists are under its influence too and have not detected it because of its invisibility.

This gives rise to another point of view. Introspection is limited on the level of ordinary thought; but it is capable of penetrating more deeply when we rise in the scale of intuitive awareness. The mind is not a monad. It is more like a spectrum. We constantly change our level of thought. When we are wholly concentrated on doing something practical, our awareness contracts almost to a pin-point. When we are thinking about some common-sense affair, our awareness expands somewhat; but it is still in the grip of racial instinct. When we reflect on philosophy and religion, our awareness expands still more. But even this is not the limit. These levels do not exceed the range of our consciousness in this world. When we are seized by intuition or inspiration from beyond normal consciousness, the greater self acts into the lesser self. The spectrum of being extends beyond the boundary of what we commonly believe to be our total selves.

This shows how it is possible to become aware of an instinctive element in us which is invisible on the lower planes where we are within its grip.

CHAPTER X

The Pathway to Religion

W E have seen that none of the departments of psychical research, when we consider those findings in detail, yielded results which were intelligible through and through and in a final fashion. All were comprehensible up to a point; and in the foreground some were amenable to exact experiment; but beyond that point the root-causes of the phenomena went off into the blue. Mediumistic communications purporting to come in direct and simple fashion from the dead pointed to the dead as being a factor in their origin; but their complete origin still remained enigmatic. There was evidence which pointed to the medium's unconscious mind as being involved in the process; and there was the possibility that the mind of the sitter also played its part; and perhaps also the minds of others. How these factors are interwoven we have no means of determining.

Telepathy appears at first sight to be a simple transference of thought from one conscious mind to another. Experiments of the card-guessing type reinforce this suggestion; but more informative evidence shows that in telepathy the information rises from the subconscious, or extra-normally conscious, region of the mind, where its original source is a mystery.

The faculty called 'clairvoyance' is similarly misleading, because its very name suggests that it is akin to ordinary sense-perception—a kind of paranormal sight; while precognition, which undoubtedly occurs, is entirely beyond our comprehension.

The physical phenomena of the séance-room, though rendered uncertain by fraud, point on the whole to the occasional occurrence of genuine physical happenings which are entirely strange in their nature, and occur according to laws which differ widely from the established laws of physics. These strange physical phenomena occur only in the presence of a human being who is in a very unusual state.

Interesting and instructive as the phenomena of psychical research are, I would suggest to the reader that their principal importance is that they turn our gaze in an unusual direction. *Psychical research acts as a pointer*, showing that things existing beyond the limits of our world penetrate into it. We should constantly look back at these experiments and at all paranormal happenings; for the important things they imply sink into our minds very slowly. The build-up of our minds tries all the time to pass them by or to minimize their significance; and it is by no means easy to grasp the importance of what they point to.

The evolutionary adaptation of the mind to its surroundings is extremely subtle, for it gives rise to convictions which are to a certain extent specious, although at the same time they are partly based on truth. Let us make an effort to grasp the situation. The external world is undoubtedly there! It is real and in its essence is independent of ourselves; there is no need to regard it as a wholly subjective creation in the sense in which Bishop Berkeley claimed it to be. But the part that is independent of ourselves is only a framework. On that objective framework, the subjective plays an enormous role—far larger than our minds are constituted to realize—for the subjective element is very skilfully concealed.

Let us notice how it comes into action in everyday life. We see, hear and touch the real world: what is subjective about these processes? There is this remarkable fact. *The less we think about the world the better we understand it.* 'Understand', however, is not quite the right word. *Seem* to understand is nearer the truth; but it is rather more than 'seems'; for the way in which we understand the physical world in practical life is in one sense true understanding. For it *works:* it renders us splendidly successful in action. And surely we must know the world as it is in order to be successful in dealing with it.

We do in one sense know it as it is; *but in a pragmatic sense only.* Instead of saying that we *understand* the world in our daily contact with it, it would be truer to say that we are *in mental contact with it in a limited and pragmatic way.* This mental contact has been subtly pre-arranged so as to eliminate difficulties which would arise if we saw things as they literally are. I do not mean that the world offers no problems in practical life, for every practical man encounters difficulties. The builder may be faced with swampy ground unsuitable for building and may have great difficulty in draining it; the agriculturist may be invaded with pests which damage his crops, and so on. But these, like all the difficulties and problems which arise in everyday life are of a special kind. They are, in principle, *finally soluble*. The artificiality of this situation does not occur to us; but it is a fact of vital importance. *Practical difficulties all lie within our mental grasp and are within our power to solve.* They are all soluble; they do not turn into will-o'-the-wisps which lead us further and further afield. They are what may be called convergent difficulties, coming to a final point after which they are settled and done with. The fact that they do come to a point never strikes us as being significant; but it is highly significant, for our difficulties would not have this 'convergent' character if it were not for the special construction of our bodies and minds. In fact, our difficulties in practical life converge because we have been so closely adapted in the course of evolution to our surroundings.

There is no difficulty in understanding matter so long as we are actively dealing with it and not reflecting about its nature. Its structure, its spatial relations offer no difficulties. Time, also offers no difficulties to the practical mind. In fact, the whole world, the whole universe, is as simple as ABC *so long as we do not ask questions about it*.

This brings us to a new view of truth. Can this everyday, pragmatic view of the universe be called 'true'? The answer is Yes and No. Certain aspects of it are specious although it is founded on reality. It is, in fact, a construction based on the intrinsic character of independent reality, and yet modified to suit our minds. Perhaps it is in some ways rather like a child's first history book. Does such a book contain true history? It is based on truth; yet it is adapted to the child's mind. But this is not quite a true analogy of the way in which we know the external world: for behind our pragmatic knowledge of it are features which we cannot in principle understand; while in history the real events can be understood, even to some extent by a child.

What seems so extraordinary is that it never strikes us as queer that the more closely we bring our intellect to bear on things that lie outside the practical sphere, the more puzzling they become and the less we understand them. This may be denied; and the statement does in fact require some modification. Physicists, chemists and astronomers have brought their intellects to bear on the physical world and it will be said that they have found out a great deal more about it. This is true. But the point is that they do not understand it in the *final* sense in which a practical man understands it (or makes pragmatic mental contact with it) through not thinking about it at all. The world as explored by scientists is surrounded by a forest of question-marks; while the same world seen by the practical man has no question-marks at all. It is completely understood by him if for 'understanding' we substitute pragmatic mental contact. This is the achievement of evolution. To sum up, everything that shows itself in the world of the practical man converges, while everything that shows itself in the world of the pure scientist diverges.

Of course the scientist goes on exploring, convinced that his explorations will end in final convergence some day. But this belief is fostered only by the pragmatic instinct which has been instilled into the human mind for practical reasons. He accumulates knowledge: yet he is pursuing a will-o'-the-wisp.

Simple as is the situation here described, we assimilate it very slowly, tending all the while to reject it. Yet, until we have admitted it, our own nature and our true situation in the universe remain concealed.

The realization of three factors is absolutely essential if we are to conceive the universe in any way that is akin to truth. The first is that the human being is *graded* and has no definite bound or confine. The second is that the world we live in extends indefinitely. The third is that the human being is adapted to physical environment with pragmatic thoroughness on the mental as well as on the physical level of action; and that its adapted characteristics enter and potently influence the mind on the intellectual level.

These three key-factors in human existence, once they are realized, create a perspective which we have lost to-day, largely because science, by concentrating on the data of the senses, has reinforced the instinct implanted in us by Nature that our senses show us the whole. This new perspective throws a different light on religion from that which is widely current to-day. It illuminates the old hard and fast division between natural and supernatural. Every race of mankind since civilization began, and probably long before, was intuitively linked with the world which extends beyond the range of the senses; and all the leading religions of the world recognize the extension of the self beyond the phase which is manifest in this world. For in spite of the instinctive adaptation of the lower stratum of the mind to its surroundings, there has always been a higher and freer phase which reached upwards and outwards 'with thoughts beyond the reaches of our souls'. There was always this contact with reality beyond the senses.

This reaching outwards and upwards of the mind was the original source of religion; and when these upward and outward searchings after the real were drawn into the sphere of the practical consciousness, they became assimilated to the sense-world and took on the crystallized forms of institutional religions. Thus a supernatural world was recognized and was conceived as being distinct from the natural, although in pre-scientific days the line between the two was not so definite as it is to-day. The characteristic feature of the epoch of science was a close analytical study of the data provided by the senses, and this examination brought to light innumerable facts about everything physical. This, in time, had the effect of producing the conviction that everything must be derived from physical sources. Thus it came about that the supernatural was swallowed up by the natural; and to-day the supernatural has retreated to the status of something ancient stored in a museum. It depends for its continued recognition on the time-honoured tribute accorded to religious institutions. In this way the modern outlook came into being; and it is very important to remember that it did so not because science was drawing a true picture of the universe, but because the constitution of the human mind, produced by evolution, was the driving force behind science itself. That mind continually urged the intellect not to recognize anything beyond the presentations of the five senses.

The truth is that supra-sensory experiences are overwhelmingly convincing to the individual, although in great part they are incommunicable in words. Supra-mundane experiences reach the ordinary consciousness by adapting and contracting themselves until they pass through the bottle-neck into the consciousness which is interwoven with the brain. They translate themselves, as far as it can be done, into the limited language that this consciousness understands. Certain individuals in all countries and in all ages have risen above the limited mentality of daily life and have realized higher things clearly; they have received what we call 'revelations'. But these revelations could be communicated to others only in terms of ideas current in the ordinary world; and these have to act as symbols. Thus, in ancient Hebrew times, revelations came through in the form of messages from Jehovah: in Greek times oracular messages were accepted as proceeding from the gods: in Christian times they lay within the Christian field and came as appearances of the Virgin, etc. That is to say, perceptions from beyond this world, when they reach through to the practical consciousness, adapt themselves to the form of religion that the particular normal consciousness in question accepts. In order to reach the ordinary mind, anything proceeding from a source beyond this world *must* clothe itself in the mind's current ideas.

The field of psychical research is similarly brought within and fitted into the forms of contemporary thought. The fact that religion is spread universally over the world and that the human mind universally draws its intuitional grasp of it into this world, terrestrializing it in the process; and the further fact that the mind is blind to this symbolizing process and accepts institutional religion as literally true or literally untrue, throws immense light on the religious situation. The rationalist, who rejects formalized religion as a product of the imagination, is in a way himself testifying to the truth of what he doubts about this situation; he is testifying to the reality of religious insight, for he reveals the fact that he is himself under the influence of the adapted mind, which urges the belief that the common-sense picture of things is the whole.

Psychical research, again, is a cogent pointer to this situation; for its evidence shows that reality undoubtedly extends beyond the range of the senses; and the attempt to reject this evidence also reveals the source of the opposition to religion.

The solidarity of all consciousness with the real—the oneness of our present scrap of selfhood with the core of existence—is the foundation of all religion. Without it, we should be no more than ephemeral and temporal atoms of consciousness: we should be what the biologist thinks we are. With it, we are indissolubly one with the whole of reality. This fact, as is well known, has been proclaimed for centuries by the ancient philosophy of India; and mystics of every race and age have testified to the same.

But, in the modern world to-day, the universal, illusory instinct, which convinces the mind that the visible world is the whole, has been reinforced by three centuries of science; and it is of the utmost importance for us to realize that the physical world is not the whole of reality. We *must* realize this if we are not to stray further and further into the realm of illusion and accept the specious doctrine instilled into the practical mind, which forms the basis of Materialism. This subtle factor in our evolution urges us to concentrate all our attention upon the sense-world as we do on the lighted stage of a theatre and to ignore everything that is off the stage. But we must, at all costs, resist the coercive force of instinct and struggle to gain an intelligent and balanced outlook from a higher and more intuitive standpoint.

Religion has lost much of its power to-day because it does not seem to accord with reality as revealed by science. The foundation on which it rests is the limitless extension of the self and of reality far beyond the range of the bodily senses. This is recognized in the west to-day only by a few. Those under the influence of the scientifically reinforced instinct regard religion as no more than a useful fiction, to be tolerated because it has a stabilizing effect on conduct. Science, because of its success in practice, is accepted by many as being the sole reliable guide to truth.

Modern beliefs are thus at variance with the nature of reality; and from this false acceptance arises in large part the state of world-insecurity to-day—the restlessness and absence of any peace of mind and the destructive doctrines arising from blinding illusions. The conscious mind is at loggerheads with its supra-conscious extension.

The reader of this book is asked to pause and reflect. He need not necessarily study the subject-matter of psychical research; although he may find it useful to regard psychical research as a salient pointer, revealing the difference between truth and the goal to which our mind leads us in practice. It is of vital importance to reflect on this situation and to realize the deeply rooted and hidden factors in the human mind which are misleading our thought to-day.

Once the universal landscape is seen in something like its true perspective, *everything* changes its appearance. The argument that life is an accidental product of material complexity disappears; for that argument is based upon our innate tendency to assume that the parochial world we live in is the whole. The argument that human immortality is a fiction, incompatible with the character of the universe, is again the result of seeing that universe in false perspective. That the whole universe can be explored by investigating the regions of space and time rests upon the illusory assumption that our senses show us the whole realm of existence in principle.

The key-factor, which it is of such paramount importance to realize, is that behind all our thoughts and actions lie invisible impulses of *racial* extent, which subtly invade and influence our powers of reasoning from below. They urge upon us premises which appear to our adapted minds to be unquestionably true, but which are, in fact, pragmatic assumptions created in order to provide us with the best outlook for practical action. The great illusion, widely accepted without question or criticism, is that human reason is inviolable and immaculate *at all levels of thought.* Reason, indeed, is not even a faculty which is complete in itself; for it rests upon accepted premises, which, in the long run, *must* be prior to reason. At the same time, truth of an intuitional nature reaches downwards and enters the mind from above; and if we rise to the intuitive level, the pragmatic and often illusory nature of the impulses rising from below is clearly seen.

The doctrine of Materialism rests entirely on two supporting pillars, both of which are subjective assumptions. One is that the embodied consciousness comprises the entire self. The other is that the world presented by the senses comprises the entire universe. Both these views have been instilled into the mind at the level of common sense because they are necessary for practical efficiency. But when once we succeed in rising above the level of common sense and free ourselves from the domination of instinct it becomes evident that the facts do not point towards Materialism. They no more point to the empirical self as the whole self or the physical world as the whole universe than they point to the planet earth as the centre of the solar and stellar systems. The Materialist has not been able to detect the subjectivism which underlies his doctrine.

The fact that progress in thought is, for the most part, due to intuition shows that the ordinary conscious mind is not a self-contained monad. The fact that consciousness is expansive even within its somatic binding, shrinking to animal smallness when purely engaged in action, but expanding as it rises in the scale of reflection, points emphatically against the view that the mind is a monad. Some philosophers, in particular the religious empiricists of ancient India, went much further in exploration of the self than we have ever done and they came to the conclusion that, beyond its incarnate range, the human self is one with the core of reality. They hold that we are rays shot out from the infinite.

This type of conclusion is not confined to the religions of the East: it is the universal experience of those called mystics in all countries and ages. The higher anyone succeeds in climbing the rungs of the ladder of awareness, the more the self opens out and is filled with knowledge of reality. This process cannot be expressed in words by our limited intellect. Thus actual experience vindicates the view that selfhood is indefinable, inexpressible in words, incomprehensible to the intellect and integral with the whole, which we can no more grasp than an animal can grasp the differential calculus. The monadic view of the self is a pragmatic illusion forced upon the practical mind.

It is impossible in a short book of this kind to go deeply into the religious teaching of ancient India; but a few cogent sentences from Sir S. Radhakrishnan's book, *Eastern Religions and Western Thought*, may serve to emphasize the difference between the view seen from a point of heightened awareness and that of common sense, reinforced by science.

The key-fact is this: 'if there is one doctrine more than another which is characteristic of Hindu thought, it is the belief that there is an interior depth to the human soul, which, in its essence, is uncreated and deathless and absolutely real' (p. 83). In the first place he points out that the Materialistic view of man—the view that his consciousness is merely a throw-off of the activities of the brain, and therefore an ephemeral phenomenon with no firm foundation—is negatived by everyday experience. If the conscious being had no background, no 'interior depth', it would be completely satisfied by material success and comforts. But that is not the case. 'The rich of the world are among those who find life stale, flat and unprofitable' (p. 80). To realize this fact alone is to see that Utopian schemes based on Materialism, such as Communism and Materialistic Humanism, are bound inevitably to head towards disaster and not towards success. A true view of the nature of man is the first indispensable for any social improvement in the world.

Given this view, the illusion of the monadic atom of consciousness disappears and we begin to see ourselves as graded beings and the empirical self as an abstraction from the whole. The higher we rise the more clearly we see this. 'Our conceptions of the universe answer to our degrees of consciousness. As our consciousness increases in its scope, we see more clearly. We now see partly as an animal and partly as a human being. Sometimes the world is viewed as one of self-satisfaction, at other times as an object of curiosity and contemplation. To see it in truth, one has to free oneself from sense-addiction and concentrate the whole energy of one's consciousness on the nature of reality' (p. 88). 'Compared with those who have seen the truth of things, the awakened spirits, we are sleep-walkers' (p. 95).

Again, the discontinuity, which is such a conspicuous feature of our world, necessary as it is for clear thinking, is a superficial appearance. Underneath there is a continuity and unity. 'The view which regards the multiplicity as ultimate is deceptive (Māyā), for it causes the desire to live separate and independent lives' (p. 94). We shall not understand anything aright until we have grasped the fundamental fact that the human being, as manifest in the flesh, is an outlying abstraction of the uncomprehended whole. The common-sense outlook might be called senso-centric. We cling to it in spite of the fact that if it is examined impartially the facts point away from it. We cling to it because it is almost indispensable for use in practical life. If the sense-world is taken to be obviously the centre and source of everything, and if the self of daily life is taken to be the entire self, we see at once how clear-cut and intelligible everything becomes, how easy to deal with. If these clear boundaries, although specious, were not made to seem obvious; if categories of external things merged into one another; if all were visibly continuous and inter-connected, and if questions once asked, were never finally answered, how impossible it would be to live in our world. Science is bringing to light to-day the universal continuity that underlies the apparent discontinuity on the surface. But it would never do if this were visible to the intelligence which is active in ordinary practical life.

Thus we see the outlook which seems so clear and obvious, so obviously real in ordinary life, is to a very large extent the result of the constitution of our minds. Even in what are apparently the most objective quests, our minds are unobtrusively operating, projecting their own idiosyncrasies into the planning and interpretation of scientific experiments. And this tendency is universally hidden from consciousness.

Once we realize that we are being made to accept things in a particular fashion without being aware of it, this automatic tendency in the mind can be seen to play its part in religion. It will be well to consider this. The religion of the practical level of the mind bears a close resemblance in its make-up to the mind's conception of the ordinary world. Both appear to be concrete and final, and all questions at that level converge to satisfactory answers. It may be based on truth, just as our conception of the physical world is based on fact. But when the intellectual level of the mind embarks on religion and attempts, in parallel with the physical scientist, to clarify the situation and to understand it better, the problems of religion become divergent and become less and less comprehensible. In the same way the problems of physical science do this.

The mind adapted to its environment creates *apparent* simplicity in religion just as it does in its view of the external world; but this simplicity is in one sense specious, although it is ultimately based on truth. The modern outlook on the world, and that provided by the dogmas of institutional religion are so widely different that they are separated by an abyss. The idea is widely prevalent that modern thought and scientific exploration have revealed the universe as it literally is, while religion is a fiction whose specious roots have been laid bare by modern psychology. But the fact is that religion enshrined in dogmas and crystallized in institutions is an effigy of truth adapted to the ordinary human mind, just as the external world revealed by the senses is a representative effigy. It is no use asking whether the Christian creed is true or false. That is, to demand a *convergent* answer. Such an answer is possible only in the field of practical affairs in daily life, and religious doctrine does not fall into that category. In religion we can have clear-cut, simple and wholly intelligible beliefs only so long as they are symbols fitted to our practical ways of thinking. If we investigate these symbols intellectually in an attempt to understand them better, their symbolical nature appears on the surface, their clarity and apparent intelligibility recede further and further away and the truth they stand for passes beyond our grasp. This is precisely what happens also when science tries to understand the external world, or, indeed, the human being. The finality which *seemed* to be there at the beginning becomes diaphanous and vanishes.

If we grasp this situation, the conflict between science and re-ligion disappears. Both are founded on fact, that is to say, on initial data which spring from the psycho-physical constitution of the human being. Both are trying to bring the unbounded down to finally comprehensible convergence, which exists only in the world of practical affairs; and even there it is the consequence of very special conditions, largely brought into existence during the course of evolution. Religion on the one hand and the modern scientific outlook on the other are at loggerheads because neither side had realized the true situation.

Within the everyday world we can increase our knowledge *quantitatively* by employing the methods of common sense; but when we try to do the same thing outside the range of common sense, it is no longer a question of amassing definite knowledge in quantity but of endeavouring to understand qualitatively that which goes beyond the intellectual scope: yet the intellect is so constructed as to be blind to the change from the one to the other. The endless disagreements, discussions and perplexities of which theology and other subjects are full are the result of intellectual attempts to pour the ocean into a bucket. This does not mean, however, that the mind adapted to its surround-ings is entirely static. Instinctively fitted to react with its sur-roundings, it is nevertheless expanded by intuition and thus can achieve a limited amount of success in its attempt to understand things which at first lie beyond its capacity. The intellect *can* widen its scope; but the extent to which it can do so is severely limited.

The immense importance of realizing the two fundamental facts, that the incarnated human being is a specialized abstraction from its greater self, and that it is adapted to react with the physical world, is that this alone enables us to see things in true *perspective*. Until these facts are grasped, the basic situation which underlies science, philosophy and religion escapes us. Accepting uncon-sciously as its starting point the axioms thrust upon it by Nature, the intellect begins all its researches a step too late. The only way of escape from this situation lies in intuition or some form of direct perception of the real.

Religious awareness is based on these same uprisings of intuition carried to a higher degree. Dim awareness of reality of a
much higher kind than that presented by the sense-world brings
reverence and veneration into the heart and makes religion a
revelation of the utmost vividness. The graded or spectrum-
like character of man, the continuation of the self beyond the
empirical self, forms the basis of religion for the human being;
and this grading reaches indefinitely upwards beyond the power of
our present conception.

In the present age, the expanded view of the physical universe,
which is due to science, is incompatible with the fixed picture
of the universe which is part and parcel of institutional religion.
The scientific view also claims to embrace the whole, and the
whole from its standpoint is an inanimate cosmos in which life has
arisen by chance. The institutional religious view, on the other
hand, is entirely a human view, presenting God and man as a
united family wholly within the capacity of the intellect to grasp.
The incompatibility of these two views has driven a large part of
the thinking world away from religion.

But apart from religion in its crystallized and institutional
form, the mainspring and origin of Religion in a universal sense
is definitely there. The universe extends far beyond the range of
the human senses and the capacity of science to explore it. The
great and central fact is that the higher we ascend in the scale of
awareness the more reality opens to us. Ascension in this way
brings direct awareness; and this is, and always has, been the
immortal road to Truth. This pathway soars indefinitely above
us; and it is the road to what, in institutional religion, is called
God.

From this point of view, the study of psychical research or of
the human faculties we call 'paranormal' enables us to achieve two
things of great value. In the first place, it throws valuable light
on what we really are in contradistinction to what common sense
urges us to believe that we are. In the second place, it begins to
clarify our situation in the universe by showing that selfhood
is not an ephemeral product of the brain but is linked in uncomprehended fashion with the core of reality. To realize these

two things is the first step towards bringing life and immortality to light.

The study of psychical research has therefore a peculiar value which is far from being widely recognized. It shows with vivid conclusiveness that certain things happen, but their origin, their explanation and their inmost character are not revealed. These lie beyond our comprehension, and the implication is that the most needed factor in our outlook to-day is perspective. The word PERSPECTIVE should be written in large characters and hung on the study wall of every philosopher, every pure scientist and every theologian; it should in fact become the key-thought in the mind of everyone who thinks at all. The scientific method has had the result of concealing it; yet it is cardinal for any realization of truth outside the field of practical affairs. Without it, we can form no valid conception of ourselves nor of the world in which we live.

The vital need of to-day is to see our world and the universe behind it in realistic fashion, unwarped by the distortions of our pragmatically constructed minds. Science, because it is 'organized common sense', has not achieved this. Only by rising above the common-sense level can a true view of ourselves and of the universe be attained.

INDEX

Apparition, the perfect, 56
Apparitions
  collectively perceived, 46-7, 49, 52-3
  crisis cases, 44-6
  experimental, 42-4
  haunting, 47-50
Astrology, 78, 85
Awareness
  higher, 76, 102, 110
  religious, 119
  See also Intuition

Balfour, Lord, 21, 23, 24, 27, 32
Berkeley, Bishop, 107
Bevan, Edwyn, 96-7
Binet, 3
'Bottle-neck', 33, 36, 111
Boundary
  of our world, 66, 69, 96, 99, 116
  of the self, 81, 103, 116

Charcot, 3
Clairvoyance, 12, 13, 62, 81, 106
Communications, mediumistic
  high-grade, 19-40, 106
  low-grade, 17-18, 34, 39
Communicator, status of, 34-6
'Convergent' difficulties, 108, 116-17
Coover, Dr. J. E., 74
Cricket ball illustration, 66-7
Cross-correspondences, 35
'Crystallisation' of ideas
  in institutional religions, 110
  in mediumistic communications, 31, 33, 36

'Daylight Impressions' (Mrs. Willett), 20, 21, 25

Evolution, achievement of, 109
  See also Mind, adaptation of
Ewing, Dr. A. C., 16
External world
  a framework, 107
  apparent simplicity of, 108, 117
Extra-sensory Perception, importance of, 9-16, 72

Freud, Sigmund, 3, 4

Geocentric view of the universe, 95
Gurney, E., in Willett communication scripts, 15, 21 *et seq.*

Haldane, J. S., 99
Haldane, Viscount, 99

Hallucinations, 41, 52, 54, 95
Haunting, 47-50
Human reason, 113

Instinct
  and instinctive beliefs, 7-8, 75, 91, 96, 104, 105, 112
  and intuition in religion, 76
  pragmatic character of, 109
Intuition, 5, 39, 75, 76, 92, 94, 110, 114, 118

James, William, 38, 86
Janet, Paul and Pierre, 3
Jastrow, Professor, 74
Jung, C. G., 4

Laws of physics and properties of matter, partial nature of, 81

Materialism, doctrine of, 82, 112, 114, 115
Matter
  insensible properties of, 62-9, 81, 84
  ultimate nature of, 68
Mental constitution
  part played by, in religion, 116-17
  subtlety of, 7
Mesmerism, 3
Mind
  adaptation of, 6, 37, 60, 63, 69, 79, 83, 87, 90, 91, 96, 102, 107, 109, 112, 118
  assumed to be a function of the brain, 39, 90
  evolutionary formation of, 96
  its structure, 71
  limited sphere of, 2, 36-8, 61, 71, 118
  part played by, in adaptation, 101
  ultimate character of, 38-40
Morel, Mme., 65
Morton case (haunting), 47-50
Myers, F. W. H., 3
Mystics, 114

Nuñez (in Wells' *Country of the Blind*), 87-9

Occult, the, 84-92
Osty, Dr. Eugene, 64, 65

Paranormal
  and normal, no boundary between them, 93-105
  attitude to, 73-5
  does it involve the disruption of physical laws ? 79

121

For Product Safety Concerns and Information please contact our EU
representative GPSR@taylorandfrancis.com
Taylor & Francis Verlag GmbH, Kaufingerstraße 24, 80331 München, Germany

www.ingramcontent.com/pod-product-compliance
Lightning Source LLC
Chambersburg PA
CBHW050534270326
41926CB00015B/3213